# Harvard
# Business
# Review

ON

ADVANCES IN STRATEGY

## THE HARVARD BUSINESS REVIEW PAPERBACK SERIES

The series is designed to bring today's managers and professionals the fundamental information they need to stay competitive in a fast-moving world. From the preeminent thinkers whose work has defined an entire field to the rising stars who will redefine the way we think about business, here are the leading minds and landmark ideas that have established the *Harvard Business Review* as required reading for ambitious businesspeople in organizations around the globe.

**Other books in the series:**

**Other books in the series (continued):**

*Harvard Business Review on Managing High-Tech Industries*

*Harvard Business Review on Managing People*

*Harvard Business Review on Managing Diversity*

*Harvard Business Review on Managing Uncertainty*

*Harvard Business Review on Managing the Value Chain*

*Harvard Business Review on Marketing*

*Harvard Business Review on Measuring Corporate Performance*

*Harvard Business Review on Mergers and Acquisitions*

*Harvard Business Review on Negotiation and Conflict Resolution*

*Harvard Business Review on Nonprofits*

*Harvard Business Review on Organizational Learning*

*Harvard Business Review on Strategies for Growth*

*Harvard Business Review on Turnarounds*

*Harvard Business Review on Work and Life Balance*

# Harvard Business Review

## ON

## ADVANCES IN STRATEGY

The *Harvard Business Review* articles in this collection are available as individual reprints. Discounts apply to quantity purchases. For information and ordering, please contact Customer Service, Harvard Business School Publishing, Boston, MA 02163. Telephone: (617) 783-7500 or (800) 988-0886, 8 A.M. to 6 P.M. Eastern Time, Monday through Friday. Fax: (617) 783-7555, 24 hours a day. E-mail: custserv@hbsp.harvard.edu

Library of Congress Control Number: 2002100252

*The paper used in this publication meets the requirements of the American National Standard for Permanence of Paper for Publications and Documents in Libraries and Archives Z39.48-1992.*

# BUSINESS REPLY MAIL

FIRST-CLASS MAIL    PERMIT NO. 1271    BOULDER, CO

Harvard Business Review
Subscriber Services Center
P.O. Box 51038
Boulder, CO 80323-1038

# Contents

# Harvard Business Review

ON

ADVANCES IN STRATEGY

# Strategy and the Internet

MICHAEL E. PORTER

## Executive Summary

MANY OF THE PIONEERS of Internet business, both dot-coms and established companies, have competed in ways that violate nearly every precept of good strategy. Rather than focus on profits, they have chased customers indiscriminately through discounting, channel incentives, and advertising. Rather than concentrate on delivering value that ears an attractive price from customers, they have pursued indirect revenues such as advertising and click-through fees. Rather than make trade-offs, they have rushed to offer every conceivable product or service.

It did not have to be this way—and it does not have to be in the future. When it comes to reinforcing a distinctive strategy, Michael Porter argues, the Internet provides a better technological platform than previous generations of IT. Gaining competitive advantage does not

1

require a radically new approach to business; it requires
building on the proven principles of effective strategy.

Porter argues that, contrary to recent thought, the
Internet is not disruptive to most existing industries and
established companies. It rarely nullifies important
sources of competitive advantage in an industry. It often
makes them even more valuable. And as all companies
embrace Internet technology, the Internet itself will be
neutralized as a source of advantage. Robust competitive advantages will arise instead from traditional
strengths such as unique products, proprietary content,
and distinctive physical activities. Internet technology
may be able to fortify those advantages, but it is unlikely
to supplant them.

Porter debunks such Internet myths as first-mover
advantage, the power of virtual companies, and the mul-
tiplying rewards on network effects. He disentangles the
distorted signals from the marketplace, explains why the
Internet complements rather than cannibalized existing
ways of doing business, and outlines strategic imperatives for dot-coms and traditional companies.

---

THE INTERNET IS AN EXTREMELY important new
technology, and it is no surprise that it has received so
much attention from entrepreneurs, executives,
investors, and business observers. Caught up in the general fervor, many have assumed that the Internet
changes everything, rendering all the old rules about
companies and competition obsolete. That may be a natural reaction, but it is a dangerous one. It has led many
companies, dot-coms and incumbents alike, to make bad
decisions—decisions that have eroded the attractiveness

of their industries and undermined their own competitive advantages. Some companies, for example, have used Internet technology to shift the basis of competition away from quality, features, and service and toward price, making it harder for anyone in their industries to turn a profit. Others have forfeited important proprietary advantages by rushing into misguided partnerships and outsourcing relationships. Until recently, the negative effects of these actions have been obscured by distorted signals from the marketplace. Now, however, the consequences are becoming evident.

The time has come to take a clearer view of the Internet. We need to move away from the rhetoric about "Internet industries," "e-business strategies," and a "new economy" and see the Internet for what it is: an enabling technology—a powerful set of tools that can be used, wisely or unwisely, in almost any industry and as part of almost any strategy. We need to ask fundamental questions: Who will capture the economic benefits that the Internet creates? Will all the value end up going to customers, or will companies be able to reap a share of it? What will be the Internet's impact on industry structure? Will it expand or shrink the pool of profits? And what will be its impact on strategy? Will the Internet bolster or erode the ability of companies to gain sustainable advantages over their competitors?

*Internet technology provides better opportunities for companies to establish distinctive strategic positionings than did previous generations of information technology.*

In addressing these questions, much of what we find is unsettling. I believe that the experiences companies have had with the Internet thus far must be largely discounted and that many of the lessons learned must be forgotten. When seen with fresh eyes, it becomes clear that the Internet is not necessarily a blessing. It tends to alter industry structures in ways that dampen overall profitability, and it has a leveling effect on business practices, reducing the ability of any company to establish an operational advantage that can be sustained.

The key question is not whether to deploy Internet technology—companies have no choice if they want to stay competitive—but how to deploy it. Here, there is reason for optimism. Internet technology provides better opportunities for companies to establish distinctive strategic positionings than did previous generations of information technology. Gaining such a competitive advantage does not require a radically new approach to business. It requires building on the proven principles of effective strategy. The Internet per se will rarely be a competitive advantage. Many of the companies that succeed will be ones that use the Internet as a complement to traditional ways of competing, not those that set their Internet initiatives apart from their established operations. That is particularly good news for established companies, which are often in the best position to meld Internet and traditional approaches in ways that buttress existing advantages. But dot-coms can also be winners—if they understand the trade-offs between Internet and traditional approaches and can fashion truly distinctive strategies. Far from making strategy less important, as some have argued, the Internet actually makes strategy more essential than ever.

## Distorted Market Signals

Companies that have deployed Internet technology have been confused by distorted market signals, often of their own creation. It is understandable, when confronted with a new business phenomenon, to look to market-place outcomes for guidance. But in the early stages of the rollout of any important new technology, market signals can be unreliable. New technologies trigger rampant experimentation, by both companies and customers, and the experimentation is often economically unsustainable. As a result, market behavior is distorted and must be interpreted with caution.

That is certainly the case with the Internet. Consider the revenue side of the profit equation in industries in which Internet technology is widely used. Sales figures have been unreliable for three reasons. First, many companies have subsidized the purchase of their products and services in hopes of staking out a position on the Internet and attracting a base of customers. (Governments have also subsidized on-line shopping by exempting it from sales taxes.) Buyers have been able to purchase goods at heavy discounts, or even obtain them for free, rather than pay prices that reflect true costs. When prices are artificially low, unit demand becomes artificially high. Second, many buyers have been drawn to the Internet out of curiosity; they have been willing to conduct transactions on-line even when the benefits have been uncertain or limited. If Amazon.com offers an equal or lower price than a conventional bookstore and free or subsidized shipping, why not try it as an experiment? Sooner or later, though, some customers can be expected to return to more traditional modes of commerce, especially if subsidies end, making any assessment of customer loyalty based on conditions so far suspect. Finally, some "revenues" from on-line commerce have been received in the form of stock rather than cash. Much of the estimated $450 million in revenues that Amazon has recognized from its corporate partners, for example, has come as stock. The sustainability of such revenue is questionable, and its true value hinges on fluctuations in stock prices.

If revenue is an elusive concept on the Internet, cost is equally fuzzy. Many companies doing business on-line have enjoyed subsidized inputs. Their suppliers, eager to affiliate themselves with and learn from dot-com leaders, have provided products, services, and content at heavily discounted prices. Many content providers, for example, rushed to provide their information to Yahoo! for next to nothing in hopes of establishing a beachhead on one of the Internet's most visited sites. Some providers have even paid popular portals to distribute their content. Further masking true costs, many suppliers—not to mention employees—have agreed to accept equity, warrants, or stock options from Internet-related companies and ventures in payment for their services or products. Payment in equity does not appear on the income statement, but it is a real cost to shareholders. Such supplier practices have artificially depressed the costs of doing business on the Internet, making it appear more attractive than it really is. Finally, costs have been distorted by the systematic understatement of the need for capital. Company after company touted the low asset intensity of doing business on-line, only to find that inventory, warehouses, and other investments were necessary to provide value to customers.

Signals from the stock market have been even more unreliable. Responding to investor enthusiasm over the Internet's explosive growth, stock valuations became decoupled from business fundamentals. They no longer provided an accurate guide as to whether real economic value was being created. Any company that has made competitive decisions based on influencing near-term share price or responding to investor sentiments has put itself at risk.

Distorted revenues, costs, and share prices have been matched by the unreliability of the financial metrics that companies have adopted. The executives of companies conducting business over the Internet have, conveniently, downplayed traditional measures of profitability and economic value. Instead, they have emphasized expansive definitions of revenue, numbers of customers, or, even more suspect, measures that might someday correlate with revenue, such as numbers of unique users ("reach"), numbers of site visitors, or click-through rates. Creative accounting approaches have also multiplied. Indeed, the Internet has given rise to an array of new performance metrics that have only a loose relationship to economic value, such as pro forma measures of income that remove "nonrecurring" costs like acquisitions. The dubious connection between reported metrics and actual profitability has served only to amplify the confusing signals about what has been working in the marketplace. The fact that those metrics have been taken seriously by the stock market has muddied the waters even further. For all these reasons, the true financial performance of many Internet-related businesses is even worse than has been stated.

One might argue that the simple proliferation of dot-coms is a sign of the economic value of the Internet. Such a conclusion is premature at best. Dot-coms multiplied so rapidly for one major reason: they were able to raise capital without having to demonstrate viability. Rather than signaling a healthy business environment, the sheer number of dot-coms in many industries often revealed nothing more than the existence of low barriers to entry, always a danger sign.

## A Return to Fundamentals

It is hard to come to any firm understanding of the
impact of the Internet on business by looking at the
results to date. But two broad conclusions can be drawn.
First, many businesses active on the Internet are artificial businesses competing by artificial means and
propped up by capital that until recently had been
readily available. Second, in periods of transition such as
the one we have been going through, it often appears as
if there are new rules of competition. But as market
forces play out, as they are now, the old rules regain their
currency. The creation of true economic value once
again becomes the final arbiter of business success.

Economic value for a company is nothing more than
the gap between price and cost, and it is reliably measured only by sustained profitability. To generate revenues, reduce expenses, or simply do something useful
by deploying Internet technology is not sufficient evidence that value has been created. Nor is a company's
current stock price necessarily an indicator of economic
value. Shareholder value is a reliable measure of economic value only over the long run.

In thinking about economic value, it is useful to draw
a distinction between the uses of the Internet (such as
operating digital marketplaces, selling toys, or trading
securities) and Internet technologies (such as site-
customization tools or real-time communications services), which can be deployed across many uses. Many
have pointed to the success of technology providers as
evidence of the Internet's economic value. But this thinking is faulty. It is the uses of the Internet that ultimately
create economic value. Technology providers can prosper for a time irrespective of whether the uses of the

Internet are profitable. In periods of heavy experimentation, even sellers of flawed technologies can thrive. But unless the uses generate sustainable revenues or savings in excess of their cost of deployment, the opportunity for technology providers will shrivel as companies realize that further investment is economically unsound.

So how can the Internet be used to create economic value? To find the answer, we need to look beyond the immediate market signals to the two fundamental factors that determine profitability:

- *industry structure*, which determines the profitability of the average competitor; and

- *sustainable competitive advantage*, which allows a company to outperform the average competitor.

These two underlying drivers of profitability are universal; they transcend any technology or type of business. At the same time, they vary widely by industry and company. The broad, supra-industry classifications so common in Internet parlance, such as business-to-consumer (or "B2C") and business-to-business (or "B2B") prove meaningless with respect to profitability. Potential profitability can be understood only by looking at individual industries and individual companies.

## The Internet and Industry Structure

The Internet has created some new industries, such as on-line auctions and digital marketplaces. However, its greatest impact has been to enable the reconfiguration of existing industries that had been constrained by high costs for communicating, gathering information, or accomplishing transactions. Distance learning, for example, has existed for decades, with about one million students enrolling in correspondence courses every year. The Internet has the potential to greatly expand distance learning, but it did not create the industry. Similarly, the Internet provides an efficient means to order products, but catalog retailers with toll-free numbers and auto-mated fulfillment centers have been around for decades. The Internet only changes the front end of the process.

Whether an industry is new or old, its structural attractiveness is determined by five underlying forces of competition: the intensity of rivalry among existing com-petitors, the barriers to entry for new competitors, the threat of substitute products or services, the bargaining power of suppliers, and the bargaining power of buyers. In combination, these forces determine how the eco-nomic value created by any product, service, technology, or way of competing is divided between, on the one hand, companies in an industry and, on the other, cus-tomers, suppliers, distributors, substitutes, and potential new entrants. Although some have argued that today's rapid pace of technological change makes industry anal-ysis less valuable, the opposite is true. Analyzing the forces illuminates an industry's fundamental attractive-ness, exposes the underlying drivers of average industry profitability, and provides insight into how profitability will evolve in the future. The five competitive forces still determine profitability even if suppliers, channels, sub-stitutes, or competitors change.

Because the strength of each of the five forces varies considerably from industry to industry, it would be a mistake to draw general conclusions about the impact of the Internet on long-term industry profitability; each industry is affected in different ways. Nevertheless, an examination of a wide range of industries in which the Internet is playing a role reveals some clear trends, as summarized in the exhibit "How the Internet Influences Industry Structure." Some of the trends are positive. For example, the Internet tends to dampen the bargaining power of channels by providing companies with new, more direct avenues to customers. The Internet can also boost an industry's efficiency in various ways, expanding the overall size of the market by improving its position relative to traditional substitutes.

But most of the trends are negative. Internet technology provides buyers with easier access to information about products and suppliers, thus bolstering buyer bargaining power. The Internet mitigates the need for such things as an established sales force or access to existing channels, reducing barriers to entry. By enabling new approaches to meeting needs and performing functions, it creates new substitutes. Because it is an open system, companies have more difficulty maintaining proprietary offerings, thus intensifying the rivalry among competitors. The use of the Internet also tends to expand the geographic market, bringing many more companies into competition with one another. And Internet technologies tend to reduce variable costs and tilt cost structures toward fixed cost, creating significantly greater pressure for companies to engage in destructive price competition.

While deploying the Internet can expand the market, then, doing so often comes at the expense of average profitability. The great paradox of the Internet is that its very benefits—making information widely available; reducing the difficulty of purchasing, marketing, and distribution; allowing buyers and sellers to find and transact business with one another more easily—also make it more difficult for companies to capture those benefits as profits.

We can see this dynamic at work in automobile retailing. The Internet allows customers to gather extensive information about products easily, from detailed

# How the Internet Influences Industry Structure

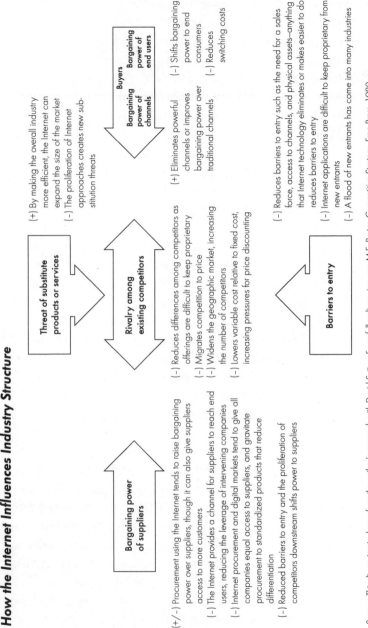

**Bargaining power of suppliers**

(+/–) Procurement using the Internet tends to raise bargaining power over suppliers, though it can also give suppliers access to more customers

(–) The Internet provides a channel for suppliers to reach end users, reducing the leverage of intervening companies

(–) Internet procurement and digital markets tend to give all companies equal access to suppliers, and gravitate procurement to standardized products that reduce differentiation

(–) Reduced barriers to entry and the proliferation of competitors downstream shifts power to suppliers

**Threat of substitute products or services**

(+) By making the overall industry more efficient, the Internet can expand the size of the market

(–) The proliferation of Internet approaches creates new substitution threats

**Rivalry among existing competitors**

(–) Reduces differences among competitors as offerings are difficult to keep proprietary

(–) Migrates competition to price

(–) Widens the geographic market, increasing the number of competitors

(–) Lowers variable cost relative to fixed cost, increasing pressures for price discounting

**Buyers**

**Bargaining power of channels**

(+) Eliminates powerful channels or improves bargaining power over traditional channels

**Bargaining power of end users**

(–) Shifts bargaining power to end consumers

(–) Reduces switching costs

**Barriers to entry**

(–) Reduces barriers to entry such as the need for a sales force, access to channels, and physical assets—anything that Internet technology eliminates or makes easier to do reduces barriers to entry

(–) Internet applications are difficult to keep proprietary from new entrants

(–) A flood of new entrants has come into many industries

Source: This discussion is drawn from the author's research with David Sutton. For a fuller discussion, see M.E. Porter, *Competitive Strategy*, Free Press, 1980.

specifications and repair records to wholesale prices for new cars and average values for used cars. Customers can also choose among many more options from which to buy, not just local dealers but also various types of Internet referral networks (such as Autoweb and AutoVantage) and on-line direct dealers (such as Autobytel.com, AutoNation, and CarsDirect.com). Because the Internet reduces the importance of location, at least for the initial sale, it widens the geographic market from local to regional or national. Virtually every dealer or dealer group becomes a potential competitor in the market. It is more difficult, moreover, for on-line dealers to differentiate themselves, as they lack potential points of distinction such as showrooms, personal selling, and service departments. With more competitors selling largely undifferentiated products, the basis for competition shifts ever more toward price. Clearly, the net effect on the industry's structure is negative.

That does not mean that every industry in which Internet technology is being applied will be unattractive. For a contrasting example, look at Internet auctions. Here, customers and suppliers are fragmented and thus have little power. Substitutes, such as classified ads and flea markets, have less reach and are less convenient to use. And though the barriers to entry are relatively modest, companies can build economies of scale, both in infrastructure and, even more important, in the aggregation of many buyers and sellers, that deter new competitors or place them at a disadvantage. Finally, rivalry in this industry has been defined, largely by eBay, the dominant competitor, in terms of providing an easy-to-use marketplace in which revenue comes from listing and sales fees, while customers pay the cost of shipping. When Amazon and other rivals entered the business, offering free auctions, eBay maintained its prices and pursued other ways to attract and retain customers. As a result, the destructive price competition characteristic of other on-line businesses has been avoided.

EBay's role in the auction business provides an important lesson: industry structure is not fixed but rather is shaped to a considerable degree by the choices made by competitors. EBay has acted in ways that strengthen the profitability of its industry. In stark contrast, Buy.com, a prominent Internet retailer, acted in ways that undermined its industry, not to mention its own potential for competitive advantage. Buy.com achieved $100 million in sales faster than any company in history, but it did so by defining competition solely on price. It sold products not only below full cost but at or below cost of goods sold, with the vain hope that it would make money in other ways. The company had no plan for being the low-cost provider; instead, it invested heavily in brand advertising and eschewed potential sources of differentiation by outsourcing all fulfillment and offering the bare minimum of customer service. It also gave up the opportunity to set itself apart from competitors by choosing not to focus on selling particular goods; it moved quickly beyond electronics, its initial category, into numerous other product categories in which it had no unique offering. Although the company has been trying desperately to reposition itself, its early moves have proven extremely difficult to reverse.

## The Myth of the First Mover

Given the negative implications of the Internet for profitability, why was there such optimism, even euphoria, surrounding its adoption? One reason is that everyone tended to focus on what the Internet could do and how quickly its use was expanding rather than on how it was affecting industry structure. But the optimism can also be traced to a widespread belief that the Internet would unleash forces that would enhance industry profitability. Most notable was the general assumption that the deployment of the Internet would increase switching costs and create strong network effects, which would provide first movers with competitive advantages and robust profitability. First movers would reinforce these advantages by quickly establishing strong new-economy brands. The result would be an attractive industry for the victors. This thinking does not, however, hold up to close examination.

Consider switching costs. Switching costs encompass all the costs incurred by a customer in changing to a new supplier—everything from hashing out a new contract to reentering data to learning how to use a different product or service. As switching costs go up, customers' bargaining power falls and the barriers to entry into an industry rise. While switching costs are nothing new, some observers argued that the Internet would raise them substantially. A buyer would grow familiar with one company's user interface and would not want to bear the cost of finding, registering with, and learning to use a competitor's site, or, in the case of industrial customers, integrating a competitor's systems with its own. Moreover, since Internet commerce allows a company to accumulate knowledge of customers' buying behavior, the company would be able to provide more tailored offerings, better service, and greater purchasing convenience—all of which buyers would be loath to forfeit. When people talk about the "stickiness" of Web sites, what they are often talking about is high switching costs.

In reality, though, switching costs are likely to be lower, not higher, on the Internet than they are for traditional ways of doing business, including approaches using earlier generations of information systems such as EDI. On the Internet, buyers can often switch suppliers with just a few mouse clicks, and new Web technologies are systematically reducing switching costs even further. For example, companies like PayPal provide settlement services or Internet currency—so-called e-wallets—that enable customers to shop at different sites without having to enter personal information and credit card numbers. Content-consolidation tools such as OnePage allow users to avoid having to go back to sites over and over to retrieve information by enabling them to build customized Web pages that draw needed information dynamically from many sites. And the widespread adoption of XML standards will free companies from the need to reconfigure proprietary ordering systems and to create new procurement and logistical protocols when changing suppliers.

What about network effects, through which products or services become more valuable as more customers use them? A number of important Internet applications display network effects, including e-mail, instant messaging, auctions, and on-line message boards or chat rooms. Where such effects are significant, they can create demand-side economies of scale and raise barriers to entry. This, it has been widely argued, sets off a winner-take-all competition, leading to the eventual dominance of one or two companies.

But it is not enough for network effects to be present; to provide barriers to entry they also have to be proprietary to one company. The openness of the Internet, with its common standards and protocols and its ease of navigation, makes it difficult for a single company to capture the benefits of a network effect. (America Online, which has managed to maintain borders around its on-line community, is an exception, not the rule.) And even if a company is lucky enough to control a network effect, the effect often reaches a point of diminishing returns once there is a critical mass of customers.

*Another myth that has generated unfounded enthusiasm for the Internet is that partnering is a win-win means to improve industry economics.*

Moreover, network effects are subject to a self-limiting mechanism. A particular product or service first attracts the customers whose needs it best meets. As penetration grows, however, it will tend to become less effective in meeting the needs of the remaining customers in the market, providing an opening for competitors with different offerings. Finally, creating a network effect requires a large investment that may offset future benefits. The network effect is, in many respects, akin to the experience curve, which was also supposed to lead to market-share dominance— through cost advantages, in that case. The experience curve was an oversimplification, and the single-minded pursuit of experience curve advantages proved disastrous in many industries.

Internet brands have also proven difficult to build, perhaps because the lack of physical presence and direct human contact makes virtual businesses less tangible to customers than traditional businesses. Despite huge outlays on advertising, product discounts, and purchasing incentives, most dot-com brands have not approached the power of established brands, achieving only a modest impact on loyalty and barriers to entry.

Another myth that has generated unfounded enthusiasm for the Internet is that partnering is a win-win means to improve industry economics. While partnering is a well-established strategy, the use of Internet technology has made it much more widespread. Partnering takes two forms. The first involves complements: products that are used in tandem with another industry's product. Computer software, for example, is a complement to computer hardware. In Internet commerce, complements have proliferated as companies have sought to offer broader arrays of products, services, and information. Partnering to assemble complements, often with companies who are also competitors, has been seen as a way to speed industry growth and move away from narrow-minded, destructive competition.

But this approach reveals an incomplete understanding of the role of complements in competition. Complements are frequently important to an industry's growth—spreadsheet applications, for example, accelerated the expansion of the personal computer industry—but they have no direct relationship to industry profitability. While a close substitute reduces potential profitability, for example, a close complement can exert either a positive or a negative influence. Complements affect industry profitability indirectly through their influence on the five competitive forces. If a complement raises switching costs for the combined product offering, it can raise profitability. But if a complement works to standardize the industry's product offering, as Microsoft's operating system has done in personal computers, it will increase rivalry and depress profitability.

With the Internet, widespread partnering with producers of complements is just as likely to exacerbate an industry's structural problems as mitigate them. As partnerships proliferate, companies tend to become more alike, which heats up rivalry. Instead of focusing on their own strategic goals, moreover, companies are forced to balance the many potentially conflicting objectives of their partners while also educating them about the business. Rivalry often becomes more unstable, and since producers of complements can be potential competitors, the threat of entry increases.

Another common form of partnering is outsourcing. Internet technologies have made it easier for companies to coordinate with their suppliers, giving widespread currency to the notion of the "virtual enterprise"—a business created largely out of purchased products, components, and services. While extensive outsourcing can reduce near-term costs and improve flexibility, it has a dark side when it comes to industry structure. As competitors turn to the same vendors, purchased inputs become more homogeneous, eroding company distinctiveness and increasing price competition. Outsourcing also usually lowers barriers to entry because a new entrant need only assemble purchased inputs rather than build its own capabilities. In addition, companies lose control over important elements of their business, and crucial experience in components, assembly, or services shifts to suppliers, enhancing their power in the long run.

## The Future of Internet Competition

While each industry will evolve in unique ways, an examination of the forces influencing industry structure indicates that the deployment of Internet technology will likely continue to put pressure on the profitability of many industries. Consider the intensity of competition, for example. Many dot-coms are going out of business, which would seem to indicate that consolidation will take place and rivalry will be reduced. But while some consolidation among new players is inevitable, many established companies are now more familiar with Internet technology and are rapidly deploying on-line applications. With a combination of new and old companies and generally lower entry barriers, most industries will likely end up with a net increase in the number of competitors and fiercer rivalry than before the advent of the Internet.

The power of customers will also tend to rise. As buyers' initial curiosity with the Web wanes and subsidies end, companies offering products or services on-line will be forced to demonstrate that they provide real benefits. Already, customers appear to be losing interest in services like Priceline.com's reverse auctions because the savings they provide are often outweighed by the hassles involved. As customers become more familiar with the technology, their loyalty to their initial suppliers will also decline; they will realize that the cost of switching is low.

A similar shift will affect advertising-based strategies. Even now, advertisers are becoming more discriminating, and the rate of growth of Web advertising is slowing. Advertisers can be expected to continue to exercise their bargaining power to push down rates significantly, aided and abetted by new brokers of Internet advertising.

Not all the news is bad. Some technological advances will provide opportunities to enhance profitability. Improvements in streaming video and greater availability of low-cost bandwidth, for example, will make it easier for customer service representatives, or other company personnel, to speak directly to customers through their computers. Internet sellers will be able to better differentiate themselves and shift buyers' focus away from price. And services such as automatic bill paying by banks may modestly boost switching costs. In general, however, new Internet technologies will continue to erode profitability by shifting power to customers.

To understand the importance of thinking through the longer-term structural consequences of the Internet, consider the business of digital marketplaces. Such marketplaces automate corporate procurement by linking many buyers and suppliers electronically. The benefits to buyers include low transaction costs, easier access to price and product information, convenient purchase of associated services, and, sometimes, the ability to pool volume. The benefits to suppliers include lower selling costs, lower transaction costs, access to wider markets, and the avoidance of powerful channels.

From an industry structure standpoint, the attractiveness of digital marketplaces varies depending on the products involved. The most important determinant of a marketplace's profit potential is the intrinsic power of the buyers and sellers in the particular product area. If either side is concentrated or possesses differentiated products, it will gain bargaining power over the marketplace and capture most of the value generated. If buyers and sellers are fragmented, however, their bargaining power will be weak, and the marketplace will have a much better chance of being profitable. Another important determinant of industry structure is the threat of substitution. If it is relatively easy for buyers and sellers to transact business directly with one another, or to set up their own dedicated markets, independent marketplaces will be unlikely to sustain high levels of profit. Finally, the ability to create barriers to entry is critical. Today, with dozens of marketplaces competing in some

industries and with buyers and sellers dividing their purchases or operating their own markets to prevent any
one marketplace from gaining power, it is clear that
modest entry barriers are a real challenge to profitability.

Competition among digital marketplaces is in transition, and industry structure is evolving. Much of the economic value created by marketplaces derives from the
standards they establish, both in the underlying technology platform and in the protocols for connecting and
exchanging information. But once these standards are
put in place, the added value of the marketplace may
be limited. Anything buyers or suppliers provide to a
marketplace, such as information on order specifications
or inventory availability, can be readily provided on their
own proprietary sites. Suppliers and customers can begin
to deal directly on-line without the need for an intermediary. And new technologies will undoubtedly make it
easier for parties to search for and exchange goods and
information with one another.

In some product areas, marketplaces should enjoy
ongoing advantages and attractive profitability. In fragmented industries such as real estate and furniture, for
example, they could prosper. And new kinds of value-
added services may arise that only an independent
marketplace could provide. But in many product areas,
marketplaces may be superceded by direct dealing or by
the unbundling of purchasing, information, financing,
and logistical services; in other areas, they may be taken
over by participants or industry associations as cost centers. In such cases, marketplaces will provide a valuable
"public good" to participants but will not themselves be
likely to reap any enduring benefits. Over the long haul,
moreover, we may well see many buyers back away from
open marketplaces. They may once again focus on

building close, proprietary relationships with fewer suppliers, using Internet technologies to gain efficiency improvements in various aspects of those relationships.

## The Internet and Competitive Advantage

If average profitability is under pressure in many industries influenced by the Internet, it becomes all the more important for individual companies to set themselves apart from the pack—to be more profitable than the average performer. The only way to do so is by achieving a sustainable competitive advantage—by operating at a lower cost, by commanding a premium price, or by doing both. Cost and price advantages can be achieved in two ways. One is operational effectiveness—doing the same things your competitors do but doing them better. Operational effectiveness advantages can take myriad forms, including better technologies, superior inputs, better-trained people, or a more effective management structure. The other way to achieve advantage is strategic positioning—doing things differently from competitors, in a way that delivers a unique type of value to customers. This can mean offering a different set of features, a different array of services, or different logistical arrangements. The Internet affects operational effectiveness and strategic positioning in very different ways. It makes it harder for companies to sustain operational advantages, but it opens new opportunities for achieving or strengthening a distinctive strategic positioning.

### OPERATIONAL EFFECTIVENESS

The Internet is arguably the most powerful tool available today for enhancing operational effectiveness. By easing and speeding the exchange of real-time information, it enables improvements throughout the entire value chain, across almost every company and industry. And because it is an open platform with common standards, companies can often tap into its benefits with much less investment than was required to capitalize on past generations of information technology.

But simply improving operational effectiveness does not provide a competitive advantage. Companies only gain advantages if they are able to achieve and sustain higher levels of operational effectiveness than competitors. That is an exceedingly difficult proposition even in the best of circumstances. Once a company establishes a new best practice, its rivals tend to copy it quickly. Best practice competition eventually leads to competitive convergence, with many companies doing the same things in the same ways. Customers end up making decisions based on price, undermining industry profitability.

The nature of Internet applications makes it more difficult to sustain operational advantages than ever. In previous generations of information technology, application development was often complex, arduous, time consuming, and hugely expensive. These traits made it harder to gain an IT advantage, but they also made it difficult for competitors to imitate information systems. The openness of the Internet, combined with advances in software architecture, development tools, and modularity, makes it much easier for companies to design and implement applications. The drugstore chain CVS, for example, was able to roll out a complex Internet-based procurement application in just 60 days. As the fixed costs of developing systems decline, the barriers to imitation fall as well.

Today, nearly every company is developing similar types of Internet applications, often drawing on generic packages offered by third-party developers. The resulting improvements in operational effectiveness will be broadly shared, as companies converge on the same applications with the same benefits. Very rarely will individual companies be able to gain durable advantages from the deployment of "best-of-breed" applications.

## STRATEGIC POSITIONING

As it becomes harder to sustain operational advantages, strategic positioning becomes all the more important. If a company cannot be more operationally effective than its rivals, the only way to generate higher levels of economic value is to gain a cost advantage or price premium by competing in a distinctive way. Ironically, companies today define competition involving the Internet almost entirely in terms of operational effectiveness. Believing that no sustainable advantages exist, they seek speed and agility, hoping to stay one step ahead of the competition. Of course, such an approach to competition becomes a self-fulfilling prophecy. Without a distinctive strategic direction, speed and flexibility lead nowhere. Either no unique competitive advantages are created, or improvements are generic and cannot be sustained.

Having a strategy is a matter of discipline. It requires a strong focus on profitability rather than just growth, an ability to define a unique value proposition, and a willingness to make tough trade-offs in choosing what not to do. A company must stay the course, even during times of upheaval, while constantly improving and extending its distinctive positioning. Strategy goes far beyond the pursuit of best practices. It involves the configuration of a tailored value chain—the series of activities required to produce and deliver a product or service—that enables a company to offer unique value.

To be defensible, moreover, the value chain must be highly integrated. When a company's activities fit together as a self-reinforcing system, any competitor wishing to imitate a strategy must replicate the whole system rather than copy just one or two discrete product features or ways of performing particular activities. (See "The Six Principles of Strategic Positioning" at the end of this article.)

## The Absence of Strategy

Many of the pioneers of Internet business, both dot-coms and established companies, have competed in ways that violate nearly every precept of good strategy. Rather than focus on profits, they have sought to maximize revenue and market share at all costs, pursuing customers indiscriminately through discounting, giveaways, promotions, channel incentives, and heavy advertising. Rather than concentrate on delivering real value that earns an attractive price from customers, they have pursued indirect revenues from sources such as advertising and click-through fees from Internet commerce partners. Rather than make trade-offs, they have rushed to offer every conceivable product, service, or type of information. Rather than tailor the value chain in a unique way, they have aped the activities of rivals. Rather than build and maintain control over proprietary assets and marketing channels, they have entered into a rash of partnerships and outsourcing relationships, further eroding their own distinctiveness. While it is true that some companies have avoided these mistakes, they are exceptions to the rule.

By ignoring strategy, many companies have undermined the structure of their industries, hastened competitive convergence, and reduced the likelihood that they or anyone else will gain a competitive advantage. A destructive, zero-sum form of competition has been set in motion that confuses the acquisition of customers with the building of profitability. Worse yet, price has been defined as the primary if not the sole competitive variable. Instead of emphasizing the Internet's ability to support convenience, service, specialization, customization, and other forms of value that justify attractive prices, companies have turned competition into a race to the bottom. Once competition is defined this way, it is very difficult to turn back. (See "Words for the Unwise: The Internet's Destructive Lexicon" at the end of this article.)

Even well-established, well-run companies have been thrown off track by the Internet. Forgetting what they stand for or what makes them unique, they have rushed to implement hot Internet applications and copy the offerings of dot-coms. Industry leaders have compromised their existing competitive advantages by entering market segments to which they bring little that is distinctive. Merrill Lynch's move to imitate the low-cost online offerings of its trading rivals, for example, risks undermining its most precious advantage—its skilled brokers. And many established companies, reacting to misguided investor enthusiasm, have hastily cobbled together Internet units in a mostly futile effort to boost their value in the stock market.

It did not have to be this way—and it does not have to be in the future. When it comes to reinforcing a distinctive strategy, tailoring activities, and enhancing fit, the Internet actually provides a better technological platform than previous generations of IT. Indeed, IT worked against strategy in the past. Packaged software applications were hard to customize, and companies were often forced to change the way they conducted activities in order to conform to the "best practices" embedded in the software. It was also extremely difficult to connect discrete applications to one another. Enterprise resource planning (ERP) systems linked activities, but again companies were forced to adapt their ways of doing things to the software. As a result, IT has been a force for standardizing activities and speeding competitive convergence.

Internet architecture, together with other improvements in software architecture and development tools, has turned IT into a far more powerful tool for strategy. It is much easier to customize packaged Internet applications to a company's unique strategic positioning. By providing a common IT delivery platform across the value chain, Internet architecture and standards also make it possible to build truly integrated and customized systems that reinforce the fit among activities. (See "The Internet and the Value Chain" at the end of this article.)

To gain these advantages, however, companies need to stop their rush to adopt generic, "out of the box" packaged applications and instead tailor their deployment of Internet technology to their particular strategies. Although it remains more difficult to customize packaged applications, the very difficulty of the task contributes to the sustainability of the resulting competitive advantage.

## The Internet as Complement

To capitalize on the Internet's strategic potential, executives and entrepreneurs alike will need to change their points of view. It has been widely assumed that the Internet is cannibalistic, that it will replace all conventional ways of doing business and overturn all traditional advantages. That is a vast exaggeration. There is no doubt that real trade-offs can exist between Internet and traditional activities. In the record industry, for example, on-line music distribution may reduce the need for CD-manufacturing assets. Overall, however, the trade-offs are modest in most industries. While the Internet will replace certain elements of industry value chains, the complete cannibalization of the value chain will be exceedingly rare. Even in the music business, many traditional activities—such as finding and promoting talented new artists, producing and recording music, and securing airplay—will continue to be highly important.

The risk of channel conflict also appears to have been overstated. As on-line sales have become more common, traditional channels that were initially skeptical of the Internet have embraced it. Far from always cannibalizing those channels, Internet technology can expand opportunities for many of them. The threat of disintermediation of channels appears considerably lower than initially predicted.

Frequently, in fact, Internet applications address activities that, while necessary, are not decisive in competition, such as informing customers, processing transactions, and procuring inputs. Critical corporate assets—skilled personnel, proprietary product technology, efficient logistical systems—remain intact, and they are often strong enough to preserve existing competitive advantages.

In many cases, the Internet complements, rather than cannibalizes, companies' traditional activities and ways of competing. Consider Walgreens, the most successful pharmacy chain in the United States. Walgreens introduced a Web site that provides customers with extensive

information and allows them to order prescriptions on-
line. Far from cannibalizing the company's stores, the
Web site has underscored their value. Fully 90% of customers who place orders over the Web prefer to pick up
their prescriptions at a nearby store rather than have
them shipped to their homes. Walgreens has found that
its extensive network of stores remains a potent advantage, even as some ordering shifts to the Internet.

Another good example is W.W. Grainger, a distributor
of maintenance products and spare parts to companies.
A middleman with stocking locations all over the United
States, Grainger would seem to be a textbook case of an
old-economy company set to be made obsolete by the
Internet. But Grainger rejected the assumption that the
Internet would undermine its strategy. Instead, it tightly
coordinated its aggressive on-line efforts with its traditional business. The results so far are revealing. Customers who purchase on-line also continue to purchase
through other means—Grainger estimates a 9% incremental growth in sales for customers who use the on-line
channel above the normalized sales of customers who
use only traditional means. Grainger, like Walgreens, has
also found that Web ordering increases the value of its
physical locations. Like the buyers of prescription drugs,
the buyers of industrial supplies often need their orders
immediately. It is faster and cheaper for them to pick up
supplies at a local Grainger outlet than to wait for delivery. Tightly integrating the site and stocking locations
not only increases the overall value to customers, it
reduces Grainger's costs as well. It is inherently more
efficient to take and process orders over the Web than to
use traditional methods, but more efficient to make bulk
deliveries to a local stocking location than to ship individual orders from a central warehouse.

Grainger has also found that its printed catalog bolsters its on-line operation. Many companies' first instinct is to eliminate printed catalogs once their content is replicated on-line. But Grainger continues to publish its catalog, and it has found that each time a new one is distributed, on-line orders surge. The catalog has proven to be a good tool for promoting the Web site while continuing to be a convenient way of packaging information for buyers.

In some industries, the use of the Internet represents only a modest shift from well-established practices. For catalog retailers like Lands' End, providers of electronic data interchange services like General Electric, direct marketers like Geico and Vanguard, and many other kinds of companies, Internet business looks much the same as traditional business. In these industries, established companies enjoy particularly important synergies between their on-line and traditional operations, which make it especially difficult for dot-coms to compete. Examining segments of industries with characteristics similar to those supporting on-line businesses—in which customers are willing to forgo personal service and immediate delivery in order to gain convenience or lower prices, for instance—can also provide an important reality check in estimating the size of the Internet opportunity. In the prescription drug business, for example, mail orders represented only about 13% of all purchases in the late 1990s. Even though on-line drugstores may draw more customers than the mail-order channel, it is unlikely that they will supplant their physical counterparts.

Virtual activities do not eliminate the need for physical activities, but often amplify their importance. The complementarity between Internet activities and traditional activities arises for a number of reasons. First, introducing Internet applications in one activity often places greater demands on physical activities elsewhere in the value chain. Direct ordering, for example, makes warehousing and shipping more important. Second, using the Internet in one activity can have systemic consequences, requiring new or enhanced physical activities that are often unanticipated. Internet-based job-posting services, for example, have greatly reduced the cost of reaching potential job applicants, but they have also flooded employers with electronic résumés. By making it easier for job seekers to distribute résumés, the Internet forces employers to sort through many more unsuitable candidates. The added back-end costs, often for physical activities, can end up outweighing the up-front savings. A similar dynamic often plays out in digital marketplaces. Suppliers are able to reduce the transactional cost of taking orders when they move on-line, but they often have to respond to many additional requests for information and quotes, which, again, places new strains on traditional activities. Such systemic effects underscore the fact that Internet applications are not stand-alone technologies; they must be integrated into the overall value chain.

Third, most Internet applications have some shortcomings in comparison with conventional methods. While Internet technology can do many useful things today and will surely improve in the future, it cannot do everything. Its limits include the following:

- Customers cannot physically examine, touch, and test products or get hands-on help in using or repairing them.

- Knowledge transfer is restricted to codified knowledge, sacrificing the spontaneity and judgment that can result from interaction with skilled personnel.

- The ability to learn about suppliers and customers (beyond their mere purchasing habits) is limited by the lack of face-to-face contact.

- The lack of human contact with the customer eliminates a powerful tool for encouraging purchases, trading off terms and conditions, providing advice and reassurance, and closing deals.

- Delays are involved in navigating sites and finding information and are introduced by the requirement for direct shipment.

- Extra logistical costs are required to assemble, pack, and move small shipments.

- Companies are unable to take advantage of low-cost, nontransactional functions performed by sales forces, distribution channels, and purchasing departments (such as performing limited service and maintenance functions at a customer site).

- The absence of physical facilities circumscribes some functions and reduces a means to reinforce image and establish performance.

- Attracting new customers is difficult given the sheer magnitude of the available information and buying options.

Traditional activities, often modified in some way, can compensate for these limits, just as the shortcomings of traditional methods—such as lack of real-time information, high cost of face-to-face interaction, and high cost of producing physical versions of information—can be offset by Internet methods. Frequently, in fact, an Internet application and a traditional method benefit each other. For example, many companies have found that Web sites that supply product information and support direct ordering make traditional sales forces more, not less, productive and valuable. The sales force can compensate for the limits of the site by providing personalized advice and after-sales service, for instance. And the site can make the sales force more productive by automating the exchange of routine information and serving as an efficient new conduit for leads. The fit between company activities, a cornerstone of strategic positioning, is in this way strengthened by the deployment of Internet technology.

Once managers begin to see the potential of the Internet as a complement rather than a cannibal, they will take a very different approach to organizing their on-line efforts. Many established companies, believing that the new economy operated under new rules, set up their Internet operations in stand-alone units. Fear of cannibalization, it was argued, would deter the mainstream organization from deploying the Internet aggressively. A separate unit was also helpful for investor relations, and it facilitated IPOs, tracking stocks, and spin-offs, enabling companies to tap into the market's appetite for Internet ventures and provide special incentives to attract Internet talent.

But organizational separation, while understandable, has often undermined companies' ability to gain competitive advantages. By creating separate Internet strategies instead of integrating the Internet into an overall strategy, companies failed to capitalize on their traditional assets, reinforced me-too competition, and accelerated competitive convergence. Barnes & Noble's decision to establish Barnesandnoble.com as a separate organization is a vivid example. It deterred the on-line store from capitalizing on the many advantages provided by the network of physical stores, thus playing into the hands of Amazon.

Rather than being isolated, Internet technology should be the responsibility of mainstream units in all parts of a company. With support from IT staff and outside consultants, companies should use the technology strategically to enhance service, increase efficiency, and leverage existing strengths. While separate units may be appropriate in some circumstances, everyone in the organization must have an incentive to share in the success of Internet deployment.

## The End of the New Economy

The Internet, then, is often not disruptive to existing industries or established companies. It rarely nullifies the most important sources of competitive advantage in an industry; in many cases it actually makes those sources even more important. As all companies come to embrace Internet technology, moreover, the Internet itself will be neutralized as a source of advantage. Basic Internet applications will become table stakes—companies will not be able to survive without them, but they will not gain any advantage from them. The more robust competitive advantages will arise instead from traditional strengths such as unique products, proprietary content, distinctive physical activities, superior product knowledge, and strong personal service and relationships. Internet technology may be able to fortify those advantages, by tying a company's activities together in a more distinctive system, but it is unlikely to supplant them.

Ultimately, strategies that integrate the Internet and traditional competitive advantages and ways of competing should win in many industries. On the demand side, most buyers will value a combination of on-line services, personal services, and physical locations over stand-alone Web distribution. They will want a choice of channels, delivery options, and ways of dealing with companies. On the supply side, production and procurement will be more effective if they involve a combination of Internet and traditional methods, tailored to strategy. For example, customized, engineered inputs will be bought directly, facilitated by Internet tools. Commodity items may be purchased via digital markets, but purchasing experts, supplier sales forces, and stocking locations will often also provide useful, value-added services.

The value of integrating traditional and Internet methods creates potential advantages for established companies. It will be easier for them to adopt and integrate Internet methods than for dot-coms to adopt and integrate traditional ones. It is not enough, however, just to graft the Internet onto historical ways of competing in simplistic "clicks-and-mortar" configurations. Established companies will be most successful when they deploy Internet technology to reconfigure traditional activities or when they find new combinations of Internet and traditional approaches.

Dot-coms, first and foremost, must pursue their own distinctive strategies, rather than emulate one another or the positioning of established companies. They will have to break away from competing solely on price and instead focus on product selection, product design, service, image, and other areas in which they can differentiate themselves. Dot-coms can also drive the combination of Internet and traditional methods. Some will succeed by creating their own distinctive ways of doing so. Others

will succeed by concentrating on market segments that
exhibit real trade-offs between Internet and traditional
methods—either those in which a pure Internet
approach best meets the needs of a particular set of customers or those in which a particular product or service
can be best delivered without the need for physical
assets. (See "Strategic Imperatives for Dot-Coms and
Established Companies" at the end of this article.)

These principles are already manifesting themselves
in many industries, as traditional leaders reassert their
strengths and dot-coms adopt more focused strategies.
In the brokerage industry, Charles Schwab has gained a
larger share (18% at the end of 1999) of on-line trading
than E-Trade (15%). In commercial banking, established
institutions like Wells Fargo, Citibank, and Fleet have
many more on-line accounts than Internet banks do.
Established companies are also gaining dominance over
Internet activities in such areas as retailing, financial
information, and digital marketplaces. The most promising dot-coms are leveraging their distinctive skills to provide real value to their customers. ECollege, for example,
is a full-service provider that works with universities to
put their courses on the Internet and operate the
required delivery network for a fee. It is vastly more successful than competitors offering free sites to universities under their own brand names, hoping to collect
advertising fees and other ancillary revenue.

When seen in this light, the "new economy" appears
less like a new economy than like an old economy that
has access to a new technology. Even the phrases "new
economy" and "old economy" are rapidly losing their rel-
evance, if they ever had any. The old economy of established companies and the new economy of dot-coms are
merging, and it will soon be difficult to distinguish them.

Retiring these phrases can only be healthy because it will reduce the confusion and muddy thinking that have been so destructive of economic value during the Internet's adolescent years.

In our quest to see how the Internet is different, we have failed to see how the Internet is the same. While a new means of conducting business has become available, the fundamentals of competition remain unchanged. The next stage of the Internet's evolution will involve a shift in thinking from e-business to business, from e-strategy to strategy. Only by integrating the Internet into overall strategy will this powerful new technology become an equally powerful force for competitive advantage.

---

## The Six Principles of Strategic Positioning

TO ESTABLISH AND MAINTAIN a distinctive strategic positioning, a company needs to follow six fundamental principles.

First, it must start with the *right goal*: superior long-term return on investment. Only by grounding strategy in sustained profitability will real economic value be generated. Economic value is created when customers are willing to pay a price for a product or service that exceeds the cost of producing it. When goals are defined in terms of volume or market share leadership, with profits assumed to follow, poor strategies often result. The same is true when strategies are set to respond to the perceived desires of investors.

Second, a company's strategy must enable it to deliver a *value proposition*, or set of benefits, different from those that competitors offer. Strategy, then, is neither a quest for the universally best way of competing nor an effort to be all things to every customer. It defines a way of competing that delivers unique value in a particular set of uses or for a particular set of customers.

Third, strategy needs to be reflected in a *distinctive value chain*. To establish a sustainable competitive advantage, a company must perform different activities than rivals or perform similar activities in different ways. A company must configure the way it conducts manufacturing, logistics, service delivery, marketing, human resource management, and so on differently from rivals and tailored to its unique value proposition. If a company focuses on adopting best practices, it will end up performing most activities similarly to competitors, making it hard to gain an advantage.

Fourth, robust strategies involve *trade-offs*. A company must abandon or forgo some product features, services, or activities in order to be unique at others. Such trade-offs, in the product and in the value chain, are what make a company truly distinctive. When improvements in the product or in the value chain do not require trade-offs, they often become new best practices that are imitated because competitors can do so with no sacrifice to their existing ways of competing. Trying to be all things to all customers almost guarantees that a company will lack any advantage.

Fifth, strategy defines how all the elements of what a company does *fit* together. A strategy involves making choices throughout the value chain that are interdependent; all a company's activities must be mutually reinforcing. A company's product design, for example, should reinforce its approach to the manufacturing process, and both should leverage the way it conducts after-sales service. Fit not only increases competitive advantage but also makes a strategy harder to imitate. Rivals can copy one activity or product feature fairly easily, but will have much more difficulty duplicating a whole system of competing. Without fit, discrete improvements in manufacturing, marketing, or distribution are quickly matched.

Finally, strategy involves *continuity* of direction. A company must define a distinctive value proposition that it will stand for, even if that means forgoing certain opportunities. Without continuity of direction, it is difficult for companies to develop unique skills and assets or build strong reputations with customers. Frequent corporate "reinvention," then, is usually a sign of poor strategic thinking and a route to mediocrity. Continuous improvement is a necessity, but it must always be guided by a strategic direction.

For a fuller description, see M.E. Porter, "What Is Strategy?" (HBR November-December 1996).

---

# Words for the Unwise: The Internet's Destructive Lexicon

THE MISGUIDED APPROACH TO competition that characterizes business on the Internet has even been embedded in the language used to discuss it. Instead of talking in terms of strategy and competitive advantage, dot-coms and other Internet players talk about "business models." This seemingly innocuous shift in terminology speaks volumes. The definition of a business model is murky at best. Most often, it seems to refer to a loose conception of how a company does business and generates revenue. Yet simply having a business model is an exceedingly low bar to set for building a company. Generating revenue is a far cry from creating economic value, and no business model can be evaluated independently of industry structure. The business model approach to management becomes an invitation for faulty thinking and self-delusion.

Other words in the Internet lexicon also have unfortunate consequences. The terms "e-business" and "e-strategy" have been particularly problematic. By encouraging managers to view their Internet operations in isolation from the rest of the business, they can lead to simplistic approaches to competing using the Internet and increase the pressure for competitive imitation. Established companies fail to integrate the Internet into their proven strategies and thus never harness their most important advantages.

---

# The Internet and the Value Chain

THE BASIC TOOL FOR UNDERSTANDING the influence of information technology on companies is the value chain—the set of activities through which a product or service is created and delivered to customers. When a company competes in any industry, it performs a number of discrete but interconnected value-creating activities, such as operating a sales force, fabricating a component, or delivering products, and these activities have points of connection with the activities of suppliers, channels, and customers. The value chain is a framework for identifying all these activities and analyzing how they affect both a company's costs and the value delivered to buyers.

Because every activity involves the creation, processing, and communication of information, information technology has a pervasive influence on the value chain. The special advantage of the Internet is the ability to link one activity with others and make real-time data created in one activity widely available, both within the company and with outside suppliers, channels, and customers. By incorporating a common, open set of communication protocols, Internet technology provides a standardized infrastructure, an intuitive browser interface for information access and delivery, bidirectional communication, and ease of connectivity—all at much lower cost than private networks and electronic data interchange, or EDI.

Many of the most prominent applications of the Internet in the value chain are shown in the figure of that title. Some involve moving physical activities on-line, while others involve making physical activities more cost effective.

But for all its power, the Internet does not represent a break from the past; rather, it is the latest stage in the ongoing evolution of information technology.[1] Indeed, the technological possibilities available today derive not just from the Internet architecture but also from complementary technological advances such as scanning, object-oriented programming, relational databases, and wireless communications.

To see how these technological improvements will ultimately affect the value chain, some historical perspective is illuminating.[2] The evolution of information technology in business can be thought of in terms of five overlapping stages, each of which evolved out of constraints presented by the previous generation. The earliest IT systems automated discrete transactions such as order entry and accounting. The next stage involved the fuller automation and functional enhancement of individual activities such as human resource management, sales force operations, and product design. The third stage, which is being accelerated by the Internet, involves cross-activity integration, such as linking sales activities with order processing. Multiple activities are being linked together through such tools as customer relationship management (CRM), supply chain management (SCM), and enterprise resource planning (ERP) systems. The fourth stage, which is just beginning, enables the integration of the value chain and entire value system, that is, the set of value chains in an entire industry, encompassing those of tiers of suppliers, channels, and customers. SCM and CRM are starting to merge, as end-to-end applications involving customers, channels, and suppliers link orders to, for example, manufacturing, procurement, and service delivery. Soon to be integrated is product development, which has been largely separate. Complex product models will be exchanged among parties, and Internet procurement will move from standard commodities to engineered items.

In the upcoming fifth stage, information technology will be used not only to connect the various activities and players in the value system but to optimize its workings in real time. Choices will be made based on information from multiple activities and corporate entities. Production decisions, for example, will automatically factor in the capacity available at multiple facilities and the inventory available at multiple suppliers. While early fifth-stage applications will involve relatively simple optimization of sourcing, production, logistical, and servicing trans-actions, the deeper levels of optimization will involve the product design itself. For example, product design will be optimized and customized based on input not only from factories and suppliers but also from customers.

# Prominent Applications of the Internet in the Value Chain

**Firm infrastructure**
- Web-based, distributed financial and ERP systems
- On-line investor relations (e.g., information dissemination, broadcast conference calls)

**Human resource management**
- Self-service personnel and benefits administration
- Web-based training
- Internet-based sharing and dissemination of company information
- Electronic time and expense reporting

**Technology development**
- Collaborative product design across locations and among multiple value-system participants
- Knowledge directories accessible from all parts of the organization
- Real-time access by R&D to on-line sales and service information

**Procurement**
- Internet-enabled demand planning; real-time available-to-promise/capable-to-promise and fulfillment
- Other linkage of purchase, inventory, and forecasting systems with suppliers
- Automated "requisition to pay"
- Direct and indirect procurement via marketplaces, exchanges, auctions, and buyer-seller matching

**Inbound logistics**

- Real-time integrated scheduling, shipping, warehouse management, demand management, agement and planning, and advanced planning and scheduling across the company and its suppliers
- Dissemination throughout the company of real-time inbound and in-progress inventory data

**Operations**

- Integrated information exchange, scheduling, and decision making in in-house plants, contract assemblers, and components suppliers
- Real-time available-to-promise and capable-to-promise information available to the sales force and channels

**Outbound logistics**

- Real-time transaction of orders whether initiated by an end consumer, a sales person, or a channel partner
- Automated customer-specific agreements and contract terms
- Customer and channel access to product development and delivery status
- Collaborative integration with customer forecasting systems
- Integrated channel management including information exchange, warranty claims, and contract management (versioning, process control)

**Marketing and sales**

- On-line sales channels including Web sites and marketplaces
- Real-time inside and outside access to customer information, product catalogs, dynamic pricing, inventory availability, on-line submission of quotes, and order entry
- On-line product configurators
- Customer-tailored marketing via customer profiling
- Push advertising
- Tailored on-line access
- Real-time customer feedback through Web surveys, opt-in/opt-out marketing, and promotion response tracking

**After-sales service**

- On-line support of customer service representatives through e-mail response management, billing integration, co-browse, chat, "call me now," voice-over-IP, and other uses of video streaming
- Customer self-service via Web sites and intelligent service request processing including updates to billing and shipping profiles
- Real-time field service access to customer account review, schematic review, parts availability and ordering, work-order update, and service parts management

——— Web-distributed supply chain management ———→

The power of the Internet in the value chain, however, must be kept in perspective. While Internet applications have an important influence on the cost and quality of activities, they are neither the only nor the dominant influence. Conventional factors such as scale, the skills of personnel, product and process technology, and investments in physical assets also play prominent roles. The Internet is transformational in some respects, but many traditional sources of competitive advantage remain intact.

## Strategic Imperatives for Dot-Coms and Established Companies

AT THIS CRITICAL JUNCTURE in the evolution of Internet technology, dot-coms and established companies face different strategic imperatives. Dot-coms must develop real strategies that create economic value. They must recognize that current ways of competing are destructive and futile and benefit neither themselves nor, in the end, customers. Established companies, in turn, must stop deploying the Internet on a stand-alone basis and instead use it to enhance the distinctiveness of their strategies.

The most successful dot-coms will focus on creating benefits that customers will pay for, rather than pursuing advertising and click-through revenues from third parties. To be competitive, they will often need to widen their value chains to encompass other activities besides those conducted over the Internet and to develop other assets, including physical ones. Many are already doing so. Some on-line retailers, for example, distributed paper catalogs for the 2000 holiday season as an added convenience to their shoppers. Others are introducing proprietary products under their own brand names, which not only boosts margins but provides real differentiation. It is such new activities in the value chain, not minor differences in Web sites, that hold the key to whether dot-coms gain competitive advantages. AOL, the Internet pioneer, recognized these principles. It charged for its services even in the face of free competitors. And not resting on initial advantages gained from its Web site and Internet technologies (such as instant messaging), it moved early to develop or acquire proprietary content.

Yet dot-coms must not fall into the trap of imitating established companies. Simply adding conventional activities is a me-too strategy that will not provide a competitive advantage. Instead, dot-coms need to create strategies that involve new, hybrid value chains, bringing together virtual and physical activities in unique configurations. For example, E*Trade is planning to install stand-alone kiosks, which will not require full-time staffs, on the sites of some corporate customers. VirtualBank, an on-line bank, is cobranding with corporations to create in-house credit unions. Juniper, another on-line bank, allows customers to deposit checks at Mail Box Etc. locations. While none of these approaches is certain to be successful, the strategic thinking behind them is sound.

Another strategy for dot-coms is to seek out trade-offs, concentrating exclusively on segments where an Internet-only model offers real advantages. Instead of attempting to force the Internet model on the entire market, dot-coms can pursue customers that do not have a strong need for functions delivered outside the Internet—even if such customers represent only a modest portion of the overall industry. In such segments, the challenge will be to find a value proposition for the company that will distinguish it from other Internet rivals and address low entry barriers.

Successful dot-coms will have the following characteristics in common:

- Strong capabilities in Internet technology

- A distinctive strategy vis-à-vis established companies and other dot-coms, resting on a clear focus and meaningful advantages

- Emphasis on creating customer value and charging for it directly, rather than relying on ancillary forms of revenue

- Distinctive ways of performing physical functions and assembling non-Internet assets that complement their strategic positions

- Deep industry knowledge to allow proprietary skills, information, and relationships to be established

Established companies, for the most part, need not be afraid of the Internet—the predictions of their demise at the hands of dot-coms were greatly exaggerated. Established companies possess traditional competitive advantages that will often continue to prevail; they also have inherent strengths in deploying Internet technology.

The greatest threat to an established company lies in either failing to deploy the Internet or failing to deploy it strategically. Every company needs an aggressive program to deploy the Internet throughout its value chain, using the technology to reinforce traditional competitive advantages and complement existing ways of competing. The key is not to imitate rivals but to tailor Internet applications to a company's overall strategy in ways that extend its competitive advantages and make them more sustainable. Schwab's expansion of its brick-and-mortar branches by one-third since it started on-line trading, for example, is extending its advantages over Internet-only competitors. The Internet, when used properly, can support greater strategic focus and a more tightly integrated activity system.

Edward Jones, a leading brokerage firm, is a good example of tailoring the Internet to strategy. Its strategy is to provide conservative, personalized advice to investors who value asset preservation and seek trusted, individualized guidance in investing. Target customers include retirees and small-business owners. Edward Jones does not offer commodities, futures, options, or other risky forms of investment. Instead, the company stresses a buy-and-hold approach to investing involving mutual funds, bonds, and blue-chip equities. Edward Jones operates a network of about 7,000 small offices, which are located conveniently to customers and are designed to encourage personal relationships with brokers.

Edward Jones has embraced the Internet for internal management functions, recruiting (25% of all job inquiries come via the Internet), and for providing account statements and other information to customers. However, it has no plan to offer on-line trading, as its competitors do. Self-directed, on-line trading does not fit Jones's strategy nor the value it aims to deliver to its customers. Jones, then, has tailored the use of the Internet to its strategy rather than imitated rivals. The company is thriving, outperforming rivals whose me-too Internet deployments have reduced their distinctiveness.

The established companies that will be most successful will be those that use Internet technology to make traditional activities better and those that find and implement new combinations of virtual and physical activities that were not previously possible.

# Notes

1. See M.E. Porter and V.E. Millar, "How Information Gives You Competitive Advantage" (HBR July–August 1985), for a framework that helps put the Internet's current influence in context.

2. This discussion is drawn from the author's research with Philip Bligh.

**Originally published in March 2001**
**Reprint R0103D**

*The author is grateful to Jeffrey Rayport and to the Advanced Research Group at Inforte for their contributions to this article.*

# Strategic Stories

## How 3M Is Rewriting Business Planning

GORDON SHAW, ROBERT BROWN, AND
PHILIP BROMILEY

### Executive Summary

VIRTUALLY ALL BUSINESS PLANS ARE written as a list of
bullet points. Despite the skill or knowledge of their
authors, these plans usually aren't anything more than
lists of "good things to do." For example:

- Increase sales by 10%.

- Reduce distribution costs by 5%

- Develop a synergistic vision for traditional products.

Rarely do these lists reflect deep thought or inspire
commitment. Worse, they don't specify critical relationships between the points, and they can't demonstrate
how the goals will be achieved.

3M executive Gordon Shaw began looking for a
more coherent and compelling way to present business
plans. He found it in the form of strategic stories. Telling
stories was already a habit of mind at 3M. Stories about

51

the advent of Post-it Notes and the invention of masking tape help define 3M's identity. They're part of the way people at 3M explain themselves to their customers and to one another.

Shaw and his coauthors examine how business plans can be transformed into strategic narratives. By painting a picture of the market, the competition, and the strategy needed to beat the competition, these narratives can fill in the spaces around the bullet points for those who will approve and those who will implement the strategy.

When people can locate themselves in the story, their sense of commitment and involvement is enhanced. By conveying a powerful impression of the process of winning, narrative plans can mobilize and entire organization.

---

AT 3M, WE TELL STORIES. Everyone knows that, in our earliest days, a share of 3M stock was worth a shot of whiskey in a local St. Paul bar. We tell stories about how we failed with our first abrasive products and stories about how we invented masking tape and Wetordry sandpaper. More recently, we've been telling the story about one of our scientists who, while singing in a choir, wished he had bookmarks that wouldn't fall out of the hymnal—and later created Post-it Notes.

We train our sales representatives to paint stories through word pictures so that customers will see how using a 3M product can help them succeed. At employee award ceremonies, we tell stories about the programs and people being recognized to explain what happened and why it's significant.

Maybe our story-intensive culture is just an accident, but we don't think so. We sense that it's central to our identity—part of the way we see ourselves and explain ourselves to one another. Stories are a habit of mind at 3M, and it's through them—through the way they make us see ourselves and our business operations in complex, multidimensional forms—that we're able to discover opportunities for strategic change. Stories give us ways to form ideas about winning.

So it's remarkable that we typically discard storytelling when we do our strategic planning. After all, that's the formal process by which we lay out how we're going to win.

At one level it's odd, but at another level it isn't at all, since virtually all businesspeople plan using lists, outlines, and bullets. In any event, over the course of several years overseeing strategic planning at 3M, Gordon Shaw, the lead author of this article, became uncomfortably aware that 3M's business plans failed to reflect deep thought or to inspire commitment. They were usually just lists of "good things to do" that made 3M functionally stronger but failed to explain the logic or rationale of winning in the marketplace.

He began to suspect that the familiar, bullet-list format of the plans was a big part of the problem. After critiquing hundreds of plans, he started to look for a more coherent, compelling way to present them. With *strategic narratives*, he found that form. (See "The Science of Stories" at the end of this article.) Individuals in parts of 3M now use strategic narratives in their planning processes, not only to clarify the thinking behind their plans but also to capture the imagination and the excitement of the people in their organizations.

# What's Wrong with Bullets?

In every company we know, planning follows the standard format of the bullet outline. It fits the way we're used to writing and presenting information. It's economical. It reduces complex business situations to a few, apparently clean points. It allows for conversation around the issues and gives presenters the freedom to move, modify, clarify, and revise on the fly. In a sense, the bullet list may be an artifact of the way business takes place in the course of strategic planning: it mirrors the character of meetings and the high-pressure pace of the manager or planner who must reduce the complex to the short and clear.

So what's the problem?

If the language we use in writing strategic planning reports were only a matter of presentation, of the way we package ideas and offer them to others, it would not matter much how we wrote them. But writing is thinking. Bullets allow us to skip the thinking step, genially tricking ourselves into supposing that we have planned when, in fact, we've only listed some good things to do.

Bullet lists encourage us to be intellectually lazy in three specific, and related, ways.

**Bullet lists are typically too generic; that is, they offer a series of things to do that could apply to any business.** They fail to focus an organization on the specifics of how it will win in its particular market. Witness this selection from a planning document submitted by a 3M business unit. The planners proposed three "major strategies":

- Reduce high delivered costs:

  - Reduce international parent head count by three,

– Explore sales cost reductions,

– Determine vision for traditional products and appropriately staff,

– Continue to reduce factory costs,

– Refine unit cost management system,

– Reduce process and product costs.

• Accelerate development and introduction of new products.

• Increase responsiveness.

What's proposed is so general that it could fit any business at any point in its maturity, and, by the way, the bullet points are not vague because we've disguised proprietary information. This is a typical level of detail for business plans. Basically, these planners propose to keep doing good things faster, cheaper, and with more attention to the market.

The problem here is not incompetence; good managers drafted this plan. They know their business unit and, if asked, could probably provide the detail to turn an empty phrase like "determine vision for traditional products" into a story about market analysis, positioning, and strategic action. But we can't tell that from their plan.

Neither can their executive reviewers. And, more critical, neither can the people who need to get behind the plan and make it happen.

But any of these abstract proposals could be part of a powerful strategic plan. If "increase responsiveness" means "improve on-time delivery," for example, it might set a company apart from its competition—if the norm in this business is to be late and unpredictable. But we certainly can't tell that from this plan.

**Bullets leave critical relationships unspecified.** Lists can communicate only three logical relationships: sequence (first to last in time); priority (least to most important or vice versa); or simple membership in a set (these items relate to one another in some way, but the nature of that relationship remains unstated). And a list can show only one of those relationships at a time. When we present a list, either orally or in writing, we leave other critical relationships unspecified. Our audience can fill in the blanks from their own view of things, or we can do it, adjusting what we say to the responses we receive from them.

*Bullet lists present only an illusion of clarity—and it can be an expensive illusion.*

Sometimes, this approach can be politically savvy, making the list palatable to a variety of people who may have different points of view. Lists leave us room to move and, in moving, to protect our sense of mastery, certainty, and control. However, in the end, lists present only an illusion of clarity—and it can be an expensive illusion. If the plan doesn't specify critical relationships among issues, it can't demonstrate that we really know what we're doing or where we're going. We can't see the whole picture.

**Bullets leave critical assumptions about how the business works unstated.** Consider these major objectives from a standard five-year strategic plan:

• Increase market share by 25%.

• Increase profits by 30%.

• Increase new-product introductions to ten a year.

Implicit in this plan is a complex but unexplained vision of the organization, the market, and the customer. However, we cannot extrapolate that vision from the bullet list. The plan does not tell us how these objectives tie together and, in fact, many radically different strategies could be represented by these three simple points.

Does improved marketing (for example) increase market share, which results in increased profits (perhaps from economies of scale), thus providing funds for increased new-product development?

Market Share $\longrightarrow$ Profits $\longrightarrow$ New-Product Development

Or maybe new-product development will result in both increased profits and market share at once:

New-Product Development $\longrightarrow$ Market Share / Profits

Alternatively, perhaps windfall profits will let us just buy market share by stepping up advertising and new-product development:

Profits $\longrightarrow$ New-Product Development $\longrightarrow$ Market Share

These different models make radically different assumptions about how the world works. Indeed, these three simple items—profit, market share, and new-product development—can relate in many other plausible ways as well. Without being clear about which set of assumptions they favor, planners cannot seriously think through their plans. Without knowing which assumptions the planners are making, senior managers cannot seriously evaluate or modify the plans. And without understanding the business assumptions, subordinates face just another list of objectives without any confidence that those goals can be reached—and without an essential sense of excitement.

## The Narrative Logic of Strategic Stories

Planning by narrative is a lot like traditional storytelling. Like a good storyteller, the strategic planner needs to *set the stage*—define the current situation in an insightful, coherent manner. That involves analyzing the industry's economics, its key success factors, and the forces that drive change. It also involves defining basic tensions and relationships: Which capabilities and objectives do we have and which do the other players have? What do we believe the other players intend to do? How do our key success factors compare with those of our competitors? Some of these factors are straightforward, but others involve complex analysis.

Next, the strategic planner must *introduce the dramatic conflict*. What challenges does the company face in this situation? What critical issues stand as obstacles to success? In some cases, the main challenge will be exploiting new technological opportunities. In other cases, it will be coping with high costs in a commodity market.

Finally, the story must *reach resolution* in a satisfying, convincing manner. The plan must tell us how the company can overcome obstacles and win. The conclusion requires a logical, concise argument that is specific to the situation and leads to the desired outcomes.

Requiring that a plan have a narrative logic forces to the surface the writer's buried assumptions about cause and effect. The act of writing a full, logical statement encourages clear thinking and brings out the subtlety and complexity of ideas. Indeed, sometimes we sit down to write believing we have a clear idea, but our difficulty in getting it down on paper exposes the flaws in our thinking.

Presenting a plan in narrative creates a richer picture of strategy not only for the plan's authors but also for its intended audience. Readers are made privy to the author's thought processes, so they know far more than they would if they read a bullet list. When assumptions are made explicit, they can be discussed and held up against senior managers' own mental models. Executives are in a better position to evaluate the plan critically, ask more penetrating and insightful questions, and offer more useful advice. As one 3M manager said, "If you read just bullet points, you may not get it, but if you read a narrative plan, you will. If there's a flaw in the logic, it glares right out at you. With bullets, you don't know if the insight is really there or if the planner has merely given you a shopping list."

A word of caution. For this approach to work, the story can't be just a list of bullets connected by "and then, and then, and then..." Rather, it must be a recasting and rethinking of the parts of the plan and their relationships with one another. It must tell a story of a struggle between opponents in which the good guy triumphs by doing a series of smart things in the right order.

# Bullets Versus Strategic Stories: An Example

A good story has a point that becomes clear through the telling. Likewise, a good plan lays out a vision—not just a generic platitude, but a fully enunciated statement of how the business creates value. Rather than reflecting an inward focus (for example, "to be the leading supplier of widgets"), the vision says how we will make a significant contribution to the customer.

Consider, as an example, our Global Fleet Graphics Division. Once upon a time, the substantive piece of the 1992 business plan for the division might have looked something like this:

- Increase our market share from 40% to 50%.

- Regain product-development leadership position.

- Increase sales closings by 50%.

Today we would craft the plan in the form of a narrative. Although what follows is highly condensed, and it is partly disguised (all the numbers have been changed, for example), it illustrates the value of telling a strategic story:

[**Setting the Stage**] Global Fleet Graphics makes premium, durable graphic-marking systems for buildings, signs, vehicles, and heavy equipment. The corporate logos and graphics we see on fleets of package delivery trucks, tractor trailers, and airplanes are typical examples.

Fleet Graphics now faces more demanding customers and more aggressive competitors than it has in previous years. Customers want design flexibility and larger graphics without higher cost. Some customers want easy-to-remove products, while others want durable ones. Bus operators want graphics that cover the windows yet still allow passengers to see out. Total sales of graphic materials have increased, but sales of traditional, painted graphics have declined due to their high cost. 3M has 40% of the market and for some years has been the technological leader.

Fleet Graphics faces three major competitors: Ameri-Graphics, GraphDesign, and FleetGlobal. AmeriGraphics has begun to expand its product line by using our older technologies as the patents expire. Its global share has grown from 10% in 1982 to 16% today. GraphDesign uses direct distribution and new manufacturing capability to compete on price but has experienced quality problems. Its market share has dropped from 18% to 15% in the last ten years. The quality of FleetGlobal's products is comparable to ours, but they sell at a lower price. Its share has grown from 24% in 1982 to 28% today.

*In short, we are losing our patent advantages at the same time that we face three strong competitors that are using low-cost strategies.*

[Dramatic Conflict] Without radical changes, Fleet Graphics will not be profitable in the near future. We can expect rapid price erosion once all competitors bring very similar products to market. Given 3M's higher overhead, we cannot compete in a price-competitive business without a technological advantage.

Our vision: Incremental product or process improvements will not solve this problem. We plan to transform the industry through several technological advances. At the heart of this transformation will be a move from analog to digital printing-and-storage technology. In addition, the quality and economics of the final product will be improved using new film and adhesive technologies. The strategy we propose draws on diverse areas of 3M.

**First, we propose a quantum change in Global Fleet Graphics' production system that will allow us to deliver products much more quickly and at a competitive price.** Rather than focus on cost reduction through incremental process changes, we have tried to rethink the entire way we produce fleet graphics. We have contacted numerous R&D areas at both the corporate and divisional levels to locate appropriate and adaptable technologies. The search has resulted in a radical plan for a new, more flexible, lower cost graphics-production system.

Many graphics will be produced and stored digitally. We will convert manual, analog, silk-screen printing into digital form by scanning the art and cleaning it up on a computer screen. We will then be able to send it digitally anywhere in the world. Global Fleet Graphics will create a central repository of images that can be electronically transmitted to production facilities worldwide. IT estimates that the system will cost $3 million and be operational in 24 months.

*The repository dramatically decreases product delivery time from as much as four weeks to as little as three hours. It also drastically reduces inventory.*

**Second, we propose development of a new generation of patented technologies and products to differentiate our offerings from competitors'.** Three such products are already in the works. We are in the late stages of developing adhesives and films that can cover windows but allow people to see out. Only the final product-definition and design work still need to be done; design should be completed in five months. Manufacturing has begun to work on production facilities to ensure adequate capacity worldwide.

In addition, we are now close to answering our customers' need for graphics that can be applied to many nontraditional surfaces (such as corrugated truck sidings) and flexing surfaces (such as European trucks with canvas sides). Films for these applications already exist in our labs.

Last but not least, new adhesives will make graphics easier to install. The Adhesives Division has a product that remains tacky for a time so that graphics can be positioned and repositioned. When the placement is correct, a second adhesive system is activated to bond the graphics in place. The repositioning capacity decreases installation time by 30%, resulting in substantial cost savings.

**Third, we need to upgrade our sales and marketing staffs' skills to match their capabilities with the technology-driven strategy.** We will put substantial effort into field testing and marketing. Technical, marketing, and sales personnel will field-test the new products both domestically and overseas. Simultaneously, we will develop and test modifications to the product as well as produce sales and other supporting documentation.

Before we launch the new products, sales, marketing, and technical-service personnel will train all sales reps in how to use and sell the new technology. Training will include both technical and communication skills related to calling on top-level executives: reps will receive intensive training in how to talk those customers' language, and they will also be able to handle technical questions on their own. Training will begin one year from now, and we expect it to take six months.

**[Resolution: How We Win]** To summarize, Global Fleet Graphics has drawn on diverse technological skills at 3M to create a proposal for transforming its business. What has been a hard-copy, analog, design-materials business will become a more fully global, digital, electronic-imaging and repository business. Combining new films with new adhesives will create substantial value and reduce overall cost in both the manufacturing and application of graphics. By these means, Global Fleet Graphics will maintain and enhance its profitability and its industry leadership.

We believe that this new graphics system will radically transform the industry in a manner consistent with 3M's overall corporate strategy—regaining technological advantage on both the product and process fronts. The competition may duplicate some parts of this strategy (for example, the electronic storage of graphic images), but that will take time. We should have an advantage for several years even in those areas. Other areas have patent protection, and our advantages can be sustained for a decade or more. [End]

Even such a condensed narrative demonstrates the relative complexity that a strategic story reveals. When readers finish the complete narrative, they will know how 3M intends to increase its market share from 40% to 50%. They will know which product and process developments should, when combined, launch a new generation of fleet graphics. And they will be able to imagine that, given those new products and processes, as well as new training opportunities, sales representatives might well improve their performance by 50%. Just as important, readers will understand that hundreds and hundreds of players must contribute in order for the plan to succeed.

In a recent 3M survey, employees asked management to "allow us to get excited about where we are going" and to provide evidence of management's confidence and excitement about 3M's future. We believe that casting our plans for the future as compelling stories can help us do just that. The ultimate success of our plans depends on how effectively we inspire the people who make those plans happen.

This final role of narrative plans—generating excitement and commitment in both superiors and subordinates—may be the most important. A well-written narrative strategy that shows a difficult situation and an innovative solution leading to improved market share can be galvanizing—and it is certainly more engaging than a bulleted mandate to "increase market share by 5%." When people can locate themselves in the story, their sense of commitment and involvement is enhanced. By conveying a powerful impression of the process of winning, narrative plans can motivate and mobilize an entire organization.

## The Science of Stories

STORIES ARE CENTRAL TO HUMAN intelligence and memory. Cognitive scientist William Calvin describes how we gradually acquire the ability to formulate plans through the stories we hear in childhood. From stories, a child learns to "imagine a course of action, imagine its effects on others, and decide whether or not to do it" (*Scientific American*, October 1994). In a very fundamental way, then, storytelling and planning are related.

Stories also play an important role in learning. Language researchers studying how high school students learn found that the story-based style of *Time* and *Newsweek* was the best way to learn and remember. When the researchers translated American history textbooks into this format, they found that students recalled up to three times more than they did after reading traditional textbooks.

Cognitive psychologists have established that lists, in contrast, are remarkably hard to remember because of what is referred to as the *recency* and *primacy* effects: people mainly remember the first and the last items on a list but not the rest of it, and—more dangerous yet—

their memory is guided by their interests. They remember what they like or find interesting; they do not recall the whole.

A good story (and a good strategic plan) defines relationships, a sequence of events, cause and effect, and a priority among items—*and those elements are likely to be remembered as a complex whole.* That likelihood, supported by a substantial amount of cognitive science, argues strongly for strategic planning through storytelling.

---

# Building a Story That Works

ROBERT BRULLO, a 23-year 3M veteran, needed to figure out what to do about his division's relationship with Hoechst, the German chemical company. Since the early 1980s, his fluoropolymer group had enjoyed a cordial, arm's-length relationship with Hoechst, which had been first a supplier, then a manufacturer, for 3M. That arrangement had worked well for a long time, but it was no longer enough.

Hoechst had recently developed a new resin, called THV, that remained flexible at very low temperatures. It was a product with huge potential. Hoechst, however, did not have the skills necessary to develop or market applications. 3M did. Simply acquiring THV did not make sense for 3M; the cost was too high, and Hoechst already had a manufacturing facility, which 3M would not want to duplicate. A joint venture between the two organizations might ultimately have made the most sense, but Brullo knew that 3M does not enter into such agreements easily or often.

Brullo thought about how to resolve the business issue facing his division. Whatever he decided, getting senior management behind him would be a challenge. He realized that a bullet-style plan could not elicit, or reflect, the serious thinking he needed to do. He decided to write a narrative-style plan instead.

*I said to myself, I'm going to write this like a book— make it like a story—so that anybody can pick up the plan, read it, and understand our situation.*

Brullo talked with subordinates and read related business plans. He wrote the plan on his own, though. His description of writing that first draft captures the painful, exhilarating process of thinking through a difficult problem:

*I'd sit there knowing it wasn't coming, and then all of a sudden I'd have a flash of brilliance. I spent two days at home just getting my thoughts down on paper. I had sheets and sheets full of ideas. Finally, I started writing out the actual story.*

Brullo spent two weeks working on his plan. Once he'd written a 30-page draft, his subordinates critiqued it, and he rewrote it more than once, preparing to present the plan to the company's senior management.

On the day of his presentation, he began by turning off the overhead projector and saying, "I'm going to have fun today." Top managers started whispering that they could see a disaster coming. The business unit involved highly complex science, and it competed in a highly complex industry, so following a detailed plan would have been challenging for the audience had they been listening to a less talented storyteller. However, Brullo walked them easily through descriptions of the players, the critical issues, and the proposed resolution.

He knew the material cold; his carefully crafted stories had become part of him.

By the end of the presentation, top management was on board. Brullo's presentation became the foundation for a joint venture between 3M and Hoechst. An observer at the presentation reported later:

*When Bob got up and presented, I could see the strategies to win. I could see these strategies changing the basis of competition. I could see the critical issues being identified, and I could see the key success factors for that part of the business. People could see the connections as he went from one section of his presentation to the next. They could see how the business was evolving, and they could see, ultimately, how the business was going to win.*

Brullo says:

*To me, the point is to communicate an insight, not simply a bunch of numbers or a bunch of bullet points. It keeps coming down to the same thing—you have to be able to show that the insight is there.*

Dyneon, the new joint venture, was formed in August 1996. Managers developing the new organization over the coming months met with far less mistrust and misunderstanding than most international joint ventures involve. The narrative allowed them to identify potential problems. For example, the strategic story highlighted the importance of addressing specific needs of users in the automotive and semiconductor industries. From its inception, Dyneon jumped on those issues, establishing teams that included people from both companies.

Today Brullo leads Dyneon as its first president. The 600-employee, $350 million business is almost two years into the joint-venture agreement. 3M is the majority owner. Thus far, Dyneon's financial and operational performance has surpassed expectations. Brullo has used the narrative format in subsequent strategic plans as the basis for two other joint-venture proposals. One of those joint ventures has just been completed.

**Originally published in May–June 1998**
**Reprint 98310**

# Having Trouble with Your Strategy? Then Map It

ROBERT S. KAPLAN AND DAVID P. NORTON

## Executive Summary

IF YOU WERE A MILITARY GENERAL on the march, you'd want your troops to have plenty of maps—detailed information about the mission they were on, the roads they would travel, the campaigns they would undertake, and the weapons at their disposal. The same holds true in business: a workforce needs clear and detailed information to execute a business strategy successfully.

Until now, there haven't been many tools that can communicate both an organization's strategy and the processes and systems needed to implement that strategy. But authors Robert Kaplan and David Norton, co-creators of the balanced scorecard, have adapted that seminal tool to create strategy maps. Strategy maps let an organization describe and illustrate—in clear and general language—its objectives, initiatives, targets markets, performance measures, and the links between all the pieces of its strategy. Employees get a visual representation of how their jobs are tied to the company's overall goals, while managers get a clearer understanding of their strategies and a means to detect and correct any flaws in those plans.

Using Mobil North American Marketing and Refining Company as an example, Kaplan and Norton walk through the creation of a strategy map and its four distinct regions—financial, customer, internal process, and learning and growth—which correspond to the four perspectives of the balanced scorecard. The authors show step by step how the Mobil division used the map to transform itself from a centrally controlled manufacturer of commodity products to a decentralized, customer-driven organization.

---

IMAGINE THAT YOU ARE A GENERAL taking your troops into foreign territory. Obviously, you would need detailed maps showing the important towns and villages, the surrounding landscape, key structures like bridges and tunnels, and the roads and highways that traverse the region. Without such information, you couldn't communicate your campaign strategy to your field officers and the rest of your troops.

Unfortunately, many top executives are trying to do just that. When attempting to implement their business strategies, they give employees only limited descriptions of what they should do and why those tasks are important. Without clearer and more detailed information, it's no wonder that many companies have failed in executing their strategies. After all, how can people carry out a plan that they don't fully understand? Organizations need tools for communicating both their strategy and the processes and systems that will help them implement that strategy.

Strategy maps provide such a tool. They give employees a clear line of sight into how their jobs are linked to the overall objectives of the organization, enabling them to work in a coordinated, collaborative fashion toward the company's desired goals. The maps provide a visual representation of a company's critical objectives and the crucial relationships among them that drive organizational performance.

Strategy maps can depict objectives for revenue growth; targeted customer markets in which profitable growth will occur; value propositions that will lead to customers doing more business and at higher margins; the key role of innovation and excellence in products, services, and processes; and the investments required in people and systems to generate and sustain the projected growth.

Strategy maps show the cause-and-effect links by which specific improvements create desired outcomes—for example, how faster process-cycle times and enhanced employee capabilities will increase retention of customers and thus increase a company's revenues.

From a larger perspective, strategy maps show how an organization will convert its initiatives and resources—including intangible assets such as corporate culture and employee knowledge—into tangible outcomes.

## Why Strategy Maps?

In the industrial age, companies created value by transforming raw materials into finished products. The economy was primarily based on tangible assets—inventory, land, factories, and equipment—and an organization could describe and document its business strategy by using financial tools such as general ledgers, income statements, and balance sheets.

In the information age, businesses must increasingly create and deploy intangible assets—for instance, customer relationships; employee skills and knowledge; information technologies; and a corporate culture that encourages innovation, problem solving, and general organizational improvements.

Even though intangible assets have become major sources of competitive advantage, no tools existed to describe them and the value they can create. The main difficulty is that the value of intangible assets depends on their organizational context and a company's strategy. For example, a growth-oriented sales strategy might require knowledge about customers, additional training for salespeople, new databases and information systems, a different organizational structure, and an incentive-based compensation program. Investing in just one of those items—or in a few of them but not all—would cause the strategy to fail. The value of an intangible asset such as a customer database cannot be considered separately from the organizational processes that will transform it and other assets—both intangible and tangible—into customer and financial outcomes. The value does not reside in any individual intangible asset. It arises from the entire set of assets and the strategy that links them together.

To understand how organizations create value in the information age, we developed the balanced scorecard, which measures a company's performance from four major perspectives: financial, customer, internal process, and learning and growth.[1] Briefly summarized, balanced scorecards tell you the knowledge, skills, and systems that your employees will need (their learning and growth) to innovate and build the right strategic capabilities and efficiencies (the internal processes) that deliver specific value to the market (the customers), which will eventually lead to higher shareholder value (the financials).

Since we introduced the concept in 1992, we have worked with hundreds of executive teams from various organizations, in both the private and public sectors. From this extensive research, we have noticed certain patterns and have brought them into a common visual framework—a strategy map—that embeds the different items on an organization's balanced scorecard into a cause-and-effect chain, connecting desired outcomes with the drivers of those results.

We have developed strategy maps for companies in various industries, including insurance, banking, retail, health care, chemicals, energy, telecommunications, and e-commerce. The maps have also been useful for non-profit organizations and government units. From this experience, we have developed a standard template that executives can use to develop their own strategy maps. (See the exhibit "The Balanced Scorecard Strategy Map.") The template contains four distinct regions— financial, customer, internal process, and learning and growth—that correspond to the four perspectives of the balanced scorecard.

The template provides a common framework and language that can be used to describe any strategy, much like financial statements provide a generally accepted structure for describing financial performance. A strategy map enables an organization to describe and illustrate, in clear and general language, its objectives,

## The Balanced Scorecard Strategy Map

*Strategy maps show how an organization plans to convert its various assets into desired outcomes. Companies can use the template here to develop their own strategy maps, which are based on the balanced scorecard. At far left, from bottom to top, the template shows how employees need certain knowledge, skills, and systems (learning and growth perspective) to innovate and build the right strategic capabilities and efficiencies (internal process perspective) so that they can deliver specific value to the market (customer perspective), which will lead to higher shareholder value (financial perspective). For the customer perspective, companies typically select one of three strategies: operational excellence, customer intimacy, or product leadership.*

### Financial Perspective

**Improve shareholder value**
- share price
- return on capital employed

**Revenue growth strategy**

**Productivity strategy**

Build the franchise
- revenue from new sources

Increase value to customers
- customer profitability

Improve cost structure
- operating cost per unit produced

Improve use of assets
- asset utilization

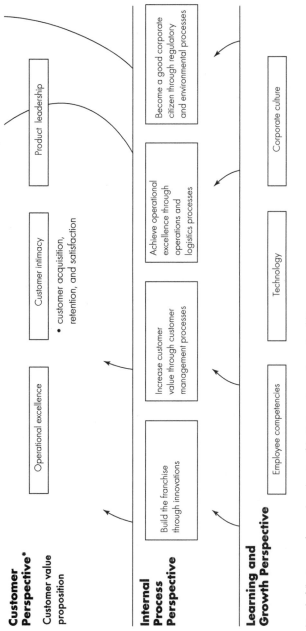

**Customer Perspective*****

Customer value proposition

| Operational excellence | Customer intimacy | Product leadership |

- customer acquisition, retention, and satisfaction

**Internal Process Perspective**

| Build the franchise through innovations | Increase customer value through customer management processes | Achieve operational excellence through operations and logistics processes | Become a good corporate citizen through regulatory and environmental processes |

**Learning and Growth Perspective**

| Employee competencies | Technology | Corporate culture |

*See the following page for an enlarged version of the Customer Perspective section of this map.

**Customer value proposition strategies**

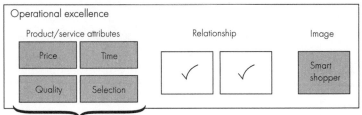

Companies excel at competitive pricing,
product quality, and on-time delivery.

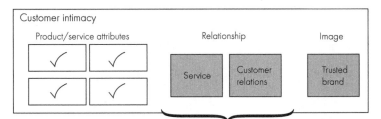

Companies excel at offering personalized service to
customers and at building long-term relations with them.

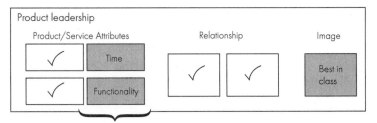

Companies excel at creating unique
products that push the envelope.

general requirement

differentiator

• measure of achievement

initiatives, and targets; the measures used to assess its performance (such as market share and customer surveys); and the linkages that are the foundation for strategic direction.

To understand how a strategy map is built, we will study Mobil North American Marketing and Refining, which executed a new strategy to reconstruct itself from a centrally controlled manufacturer of commodity products to a decentralized, customer-driven organization. As a result, Mobil increased its operating cash flow by more than $1 billion per year and became the industry's profit leader.

# From the Top Down

The best way to build strategy maps is from the top down, starting with the destination and then charting the routes that will lead there. Corporate executives should first review their mission statement and their core values—why their company exists and what it believes in. With that information, managers can develop a strategic vision, or what the company wants to become. This vision should create a clear picture of the company's overall goal—for example, to become the profit leader in an industry. A strategy must then define the logic of how to arrive at that destination.

### FINANCIAL PERSPECTIVE

Building a strategy map typically starts with a financial strategy for increasing shareholder value. (Nonprofit and government units often place their customers or constituents—not the financials—at the top of their strategy maps.) Companies have two basic levers for their financial strategy: revenue growth and productivity. The former generally has two components: build the franchise with revenue from new markets, new products, and new customers; and increase value to existing customers by deepening relationships with them through expanded sales—for example, cross-selling products or offering bundled products instead of single products. The productivity strategy also usually has two parts: improve the company's cost structure by reducing direct and indirect expenses, and use assets more efficiently by reducing the working and fixed capital needed to support a given level of business.

In general, the productivity strategy yields results sooner than the growth strategy. But one of the principal contributions of a strategy map is to highlight the opportunities for enhancing financial performance through revenue growth, not just by cost reduction and improved asset utilization. Also, balancing the two strategies helps to ensure that cost and asset reductions do not compromise a company's growth opportunities with customers.

Mobil's stated strategic vision was "to be the best integrated refiner-marketer in the United States by efficiently delivering unprecedented value to customers." The company's high-level financial goal was to increase its return on capital employed by more than six percentage points within three years. To achieve that, executives used all four of the drivers of a financial strategy that we break out in the strategy map—two for revenue growth and two for productivity. (See the financial portion of the exhibit "Mobil's Strategy Map.")

The revenue growth strategy called for Mobil to expand sales outside of gasoline by offering convenience store products and services, ancillary automotive services (car washes, oil changes, and minor repairs), automotive products (oil, antifreeze, and wiper fluid), and common replacement parts (tires and wiper blades). Also, the company would sell more premium brands to customers, and it would increase sales faster than the industry average. In terms of productivity, Mobil wanted to slash operating expenses per gallon sold to the lowest level in the industry and extract more from existing assets—for example, by reducing the downtime at its oil refineries and increasing their yields.

## CUSTOMER PERSPECTIVE

The core of any business strategy is the customer value proposition, which describes the unique mix of product and service attributes, customer relations, and corporate image that a company offers. It defines how the organization will differentiate itself from competitors to attract, retain, and deepen relationships with targeted

---

### Mobil's Strategy Map

*Shown on pages 82 and 83 is a map for the strategy that Mobil North American Marketing and Refining used to transform itself from a centrally controlled manufacturer of commodity products to a decentralized customer-driven organization. A major part of the strategy was to target consumers who were willing to pay price premiums for gasoline if they could buy at fast, friendly stations that were outfitted with excellent convenience stores. Their purchases enabled Mobil to increase its profit margins and its revenue from nongasoline products. Using the strategy map shown here, Mobil increased its operating cash flow by more than $1 billion per year.*

 general requirement

▨ differentiator

• measure of achievement

\*\*To account for Mobil's independent-dealer customers—not just consumers—the company adapted the strategy map template to factor in dealer relationships.

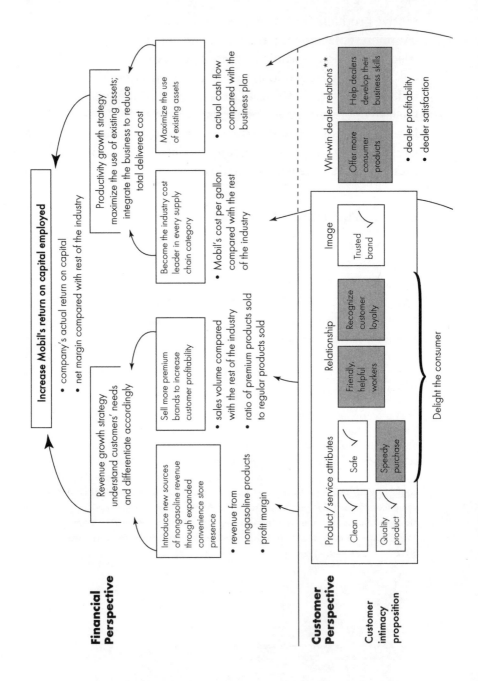

**Financial Perspective**

**Increase Mobil's return on capital employed**
- company's actual return on capital
- net margin compared with rest of the industry

**Revenue growth strategy**
understand customers' needs and differentiate accordingly

Introduce new sources of nongasoline revenue through expanded convenience store presence
- revenue from nongasoline products
- profit margin

Sell more premium brands to increase customer profitability
- sales volume compared with the rest of the industry
- ratio of premium products sold to regular products sold

**Productivity growth strategy**
maximize the use of existing assets; integrate the business to reduce total delivered cost

Become the industry cost leader in every supply chain category
- Mobil's cost per gallon compared with the rest of the industry

Maximize the use of existing assets
- actual cash flow compared with the business plan

Win-win dealer relations**
- Offer more consumer products
- Help dealers develop their business skills
- dealer profitability
- dealer satisfaction

**Customer Perspective**

**Customer intimacy proposition**

Product / service attributes

Clean   Safe   Quality product   Speedy purchase

Relationship

Friendly, helpful workers   Recognize customer loyalty

Image

Trusted brand

Delight the consumer

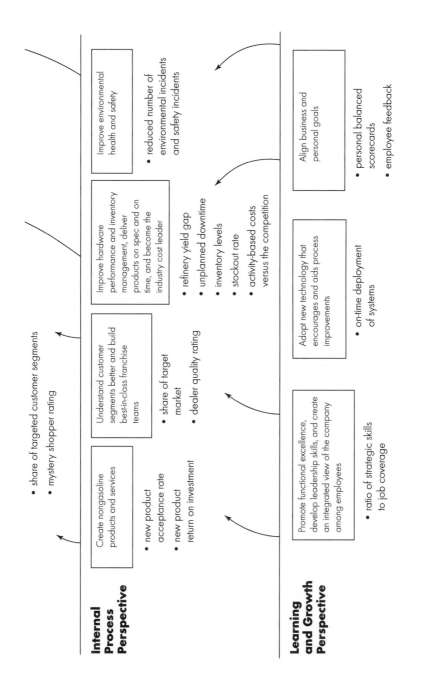

**Internal Process Perspective**

- share of targeted customer segments
- mystery shopper rating

Create nongasoline products and services

- new product acceptance rate
- new product return on investment

Understand customer segments better and build best-in-class franchise teams

- share of target market
- dealer quality rating

Improve hardware performance and inventory management, deliver products on spec and on time, and become the industry cost leader

- refinery yield gap
- unplanned downtime
- inventory levels
- stockout rate
- activity-based costs versus the competition

Improve environmental health and safety

- reduced number of environmental incidents and safety incidents

**Learning and Growth Perspective**

Promote functional excellence, develop leadership skills, and create an integrated view of the company among employees

- ratio of strategic skills to job coverage

Adopt new technology that encourages and aids process improvements

- on-time deployment of systems

Align business and personal goals

- personal balanced scorecards
- employee feedback

customers. The value proposition is crucial because it helps an organization connect its internal processes to improved outcomes with its customers.

Typically, the value proposition is chosen from among three differentiators: operational excellence (for example, McDonald's and Dell Computer), customer intimacy (for example, Home Depot and IBM in the 1960s and 1970s), and product leadership (for example, Intel and Sony).[2] Companies strive to excel in one of the three areas while maintaining threshold standards in the other two. By identifying its customer value proposition, a company will then know which classes and types of customers to target. In our research, we have found that although a clear definition of the value proposition is the single most important step in developing a strategy, approximately three-quarters of executive teams do not have consensus about this basic information.

The inset of the exhibit "The Balanced Scorecard Strategy Map" highlights the different objectives for the three generic strategy concepts of operational excellence, customer intimacy, and product leadership. Specifically, companies that pursue a strategy of operational excellence need to excel at competitive pricing, product quality and selection, speedy order fulfillment, and on-time delivery. For customer intimacy, an organization must stress the quality of its relationships with customers, including exceptional service and the completeness of the solutions it offers. And companies that pursue a product leadership strategy must concentrate on the functionality, features, and overall performance of its products or services.

Mobil, in the past, had attempted to sell a full range of products and services to all consumers, while still matching the low prices of nearby discount stations. But this unfocused strategy had failed, leading to poor financial performance in the early '90s. Through market research, Mobil discovered that price-sensitive consumers represented only about 20% of gasoline purchasers, while consumer segments representing nearly 60% of the market might be willing to pay significant price premiums for gasoline if they could buy at stations that were fast, friendly, and outfitted with excellent convenience stores. With this information, Mobil made the crucial decision to adopt a "differentiated value proposition." The company would target the premium customer segments by offering them immediate access to gasoline pumps, each equipped with a self-payment mechanism; safe, well-lit stations; clean restrooms; convenience stores stocked with fresh, high-quality merchandise; and friendly employees.

Mobil decided that the consumer's buying experience was so central to its strategy that it invested in a new system for measuring its progress in this area. Each month, the company sent "mystery shoppers" to purchase fuel and a snack at every Mobil station nationwide and then asked the shoppers to evaluate their buying experience based on 23 specific criteria. Thus, Mobil could use a fairly simple set of metrics (share of targeted customer segments and a summary score from the mystery shoppers) for its consumer objectives.

But Mobil does not sell directly to consumers. The company's immediate customers are the independent owners of gasoline stations. These franchised retailers purchase gasoline and other products from Mobil and sell them to consumers in Mobil-branded stations. Because dealers were such a critical part of the new strategy, Mobil included two additional metrics to its customer perspective: dealer profitability and dealer satisfaction.

Thus, Mobil's complete customer strategy motivated independent dealers to deliver a great buying experience that would attract an increasing share of targeted consumers. These consumers would buy products and services at premium prices, increasing profits for both Mobil and its dealers, who would then continue to be motivated to offer the great buying experience. And this virtuous cycle would generate the revenue growth for Mobil's financial strategy. Note that the objectives in the customer perspective portion of Mobil's strategy map were not generic, undifferentiated items like "customer satisfaction." Instead, they were specific and focused on the company's strategy.

### INTERNAL PROCESS PERSPECTIVE

Once an organization has a clear picture of its customer and financial perspectives, it can then determine the means by which it will achieve the differentiated value proposition for customers and the productivity improvements to reach its financial objectives. The internal process perspective captures these critical organizational activities, which fall into four high-level processes: build the franchise by innovating with new products and services and by penetrating new markets and customer segments; increase customer value by deepening relationships with existing customers; achieve operational excellence by improving supply chain management, the cost, quality, and cycle time of internal processes, asset utilization, and capacity management; and become a good corporate citizen by establishing effective relationships with external stakeholders.

An important caveat to remember here is that while many companies espouse a strategy that calls for innovation or for developing value-adding customer relationships, they mistakenly choose to measure only the cost and quality of their operations—and not their innovations or their customer management processes. These companies have a complete disconnect between their strategy and how they measure it. Not surprisingly, these organizations typically have great difficulty implementing their growth strategies.

The financial benefits from improved business processes typically reveal themselves in stages. Cost savings from increased operational efficiencies and process improvements create short-term benefits. Revenue growth from enhanced customer relationships accrues in the intermediate term. And increased innovation can produce long-term revenue and margin improvements.

Thus, a complete strategy should involve generating returns from all three of these internal processes. (See the internal process portion of the exhibit "Mobil's Strategy Map.")

Mobil's internal process objectives included building the franchise by developing new products and services, such as sales from convenience stores; and enhancing customer value by training dealers to become better managers and by helping them generate profits from nongasoline products and services. The plan was that if dealers could capture increased revenues and profits from products other than gasoline, they could then rely less on gasoline sales, allowing Mobil to capture a larger profit share of its sales of gasoline to dealers.

For its customer intimacy strategy, Mobil had to excel at understanding its consumer segments. And because Mobil doesn't sell directly to consumers, the company also had to concentrate on building best-in-class franchise teams.

Interestingly, Mobil placed a heavy emphasis on objectives to improve its basic refining and distribution operations, such as lowering operating costs, reducing the downtime of equipment, and improving product quality and the number of on-time deliveries.

When a company such as Mobil adopts a customer intimacy strategy, it usually focuses on its customer management processes. But Mobil's differentiation occurred at the dealer locations, not at its own facilities, which basically produced commodity products (gasoline, heating oil, and jet fuel). So Mobil could not charge its dealers higher prices to make up for any higher costs incurred in its basic manufacturing and distribution operations. Consequently, the company had to focus heavily on achieving operational excellence throughout its value chain of operations.

Finally, as part of both its operational-excellence and corporate-citizen themes, Mobil wanted to eliminate environmental and safety accidents. Executives believed that if there were injuries and other problems at work, then employees were probably not paying sufficient attention to their jobs.

## LEARNING AND GROWTH PERSPECTIVE

The foundation of any strategy map is the learning and growth perspective, which defines the core competencies and skills, the technologies, and the corporate culture needed to support an organization's strategy. These objectives enable a company to align its human resources and information technology with its strategy. Specifically, the organization must determine how it will satisfy the requirements from critical internal processes, the differentiated value proposition, and customer relationships. Although executive teams readily acknowledge the importance of the learning and growth perspective, they generally have trouble defining the corresponding objectives.

Mobil identified that its employees needed to gain a broader understanding of the marketing and refining business from end to end. Additionally, the company knew it had to nurture the leadership skills that were necessary for its managers to articulate the company's vision and develop employees. Mobil identified key technologies that it had to develop, including automated equipment for monitoring the refining processes and extensive databases and tools to analyze consumers' buying experiences.

Upon completing its learning and growth perspective, Mobil now had a complete strategy map linked across the four major perspectives, from which Mobil's different business units and service departments could develop their own detailed maps for their respective operations. This process helped the company detect and fill major gaps in the strategies being implemented at lower levels of the organization. For example, senior management noticed that one business unit had no objectives or metrics for dealers (see the exhibit "What's Missing?"). Had this unit discovered how to bypass dealers and sell gasoline directly to consumers? Were dealer relationships no longer strategic for this unit? Another business unit had no measure for quality. Had the unit achieved perfection? Strategy maps can help uncover and remedy such omissions.

Strategy maps also help identify when scorecards are not truly strategic. Many organizations have built stakeholder scorecards, not strategy scorecards, by developing a seemingly balanced measurement system around three dominant groups of constituents: employees, customers, and shareholders. A strategy, however, must describe *how* a company will achieve its desired outcome of satisfying employees, customers, and shareholders. The "how" must include the value proposition in the customer perspective; the innovation, customer management, and operating processes in the internal process perspective; and the employee skills and information technology capabilities in the learning and growth perspective. These elements are as fundamental to the strategy as the projected outcome of the strategy.

Another limitation occurs when companies build key performance indicator (KPI) scorecards. For example, one financial services organization identified the four Ps in its balanced scorecard: profits, portfolio (the volume of loans), process (the percentage of processes that are ISO certified), and people (the diversity of new employees). Although this approach was more balanced than using just financial measures, a comparison of the four Ps with a strategy map revealed several missing components: no customer measures, only a single internal-process metric—which was focused on an initiative, not an outcome—and no defined role for information technology, a strange omission for a financial services organization. In actuality, KPI scorecards are an ad hoc collection of measures, a checklist, or perhaps elements in a compensation plan, but they don't describe a coherent strategy. Unless the link to strategy has been clearly thought through, a KPI scorecard can be a dangerous illusion.

Perhaps the greatest benefit of strategy maps is their ability to communicate strategy to an entire organization.

## What's Missing?

*Strategy maps can help a company detect major gaps in the strategies being implemented at lower levels in the organization. At Mobil, senior managers noticed that one business unit had no objectives or metrics for dealers, as shown below left. Had this unit discovered how to bypass Mobil dealers and sell gasoline directly to consumers? Another business unit had no measure for quality, as shown below right. Had this unit somehow perfected its operations?*

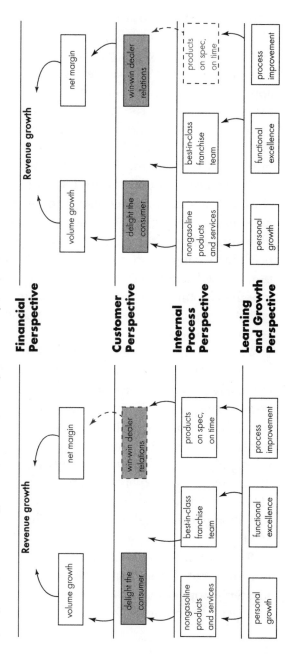

**Financial Perspective**

Revenue growth

volume growth → net margin

**Customer Perspective**

delight the consumer — win-win dealer relations

**Internal Process Perspective**

nongasoline products and services — best-in-class franchise team — products on spec, on time

**Learning and Growth Perspective**

personal growth — functional excellence — process improvement

The power of doing so is amply demonstrated by the story of how Mobil developed Speedpass, a small device carried on a keychain that, when waved in front of a photocell on a gasoline pump, identifies the consumer and charges the appropriate credit or debit card for the purchase. The idea for Speedpass came from a planning manager in the marketing technology group who learned from Mobil's balanced scorecard about the importance of speed in the purchasing transaction. He came up with the concept of a device that could automatically handle the entire purchasing transaction. He worked with a gasoline-pump manufacturer and a semiconductor company to turn that idea into reality. After its introduction, Speedpass soon became a strong differentiator for Mobil's value proposition of fast, friendly service. From 1997 on, executives modified Mobil's balanced scorecard to include new objectives for the number of consumers and dealers that adopted Speedpass.

With all its employees now aligned to the new strategy, Mobil North American Marketing and Refining executed a remarkable turnaround in less than two years to become the industry's profit leader from 1995 up through its merger with Exxon in late 1999. The division increased its return on capital employed from 6% to 16%; sales growth exceeded the industry average by more than 2% annually; cash expenses decreased by 20%; and in 1998, the division's operating cash flow was more than $1 billion per year higher than at the launch of the new strategy.

These impressive financial results were driven by improvements throughout Mobil's strategy map: mystery-shopper scores and dealer quality increased each year; the number of consumers using Speedpass grew by one million annually; environmental and safety accidents plunged between 60% and 80%; lost oil-refinery yields due to systems downtime dropped by 70%; and employee awareness and commitment to the strategy more than quadrupled.

## Not an Art Form

We do not claim to have made a science of strategy; the formulation of great strategies is an art, and it will always remain so. But the description of strategy should not be an art. If people can describe strategy in a more disciplined way, they will increase the likelihood of its successful implementation. Strategy maps will help organizations view their strategies in a cohesive, inte-grated, and systematic way. They often expose gaps in strategies, enabling executives to take early corrective actions. Executives can also use the maps as the foun-dation for a management system that can help an orga-nization implement its growth initiatives effectively and rapidly.

Strategy implies the movement of an organization from its present position to a desirable but uncertain future position. Because the organization has never been to this future place, the pathway to it consists of a series of linked hypotheses. A strategy map specifies these cause-and-effect relationships, which makes them explicit and testable. The key, then, to implementing strategy is to have everyone in the organization clearly understand the underlying hypotheses, to align all orga-nizational units and resources with those hypotheses, to test the hypotheses continually, and to use those results to adapt as required.

# Notes

1. See Robert S. Kaplan and David P. Norton's *The Balanced Scorecard: Translating Strategy into Action* (Harvard Business School Press, 1996).

2. These three generic value propositions were initially articulated in Michael Treacy and Fred Wiersema's *The Discipline of Market Leaders* (Addison-Wesley, 1995).

Originally published in September–October 2000
Reprint R00509

# Strategy as Simple Rules

KATHLEEN M. EISENHARDT AND

DONALD N. SULL

## Executive Summary

THE SUCCESS OF YAHOO!, eBay, Enron, and other
companies that have become adept at morphing to meet
the demands of changing markets can't be explained
using traditional thinking about competitive strategy.
These companies have succeeded by pursuing constantly
evolving strategies in market spaces that were considered
unattractive according to traditional measures.

In this article—the third in an HBR series by Kathleen
Eisenhardt and Donald Sull on strategy in the new economy—the authors ask, what are the sources of competitive advantage in high-velocity markets? The secret, they
say, is strategy as simple rules. The companies know that
the greatest opportunities for competitive advantage lie
in market confusion, but they recognize the need for a
few crucial strategic processes and a few simple rules. In

traditional strategy, advantage comes from exploiting resources or stable market positions. In strategy as simple rules, advantage comes from successfully seizing fleeting opportunities.

Key strategic processes, such as product innovation, partnering, or spinout creation, place the company where the flow of opportunities is greatest. Simple rules then provide the guidelines within which managers can pursue such opportunities. Simple rules, which grow out of experience, fall into five broad categories: how-to rules, boundary conditions, priority rules, timing rules, and exit rules. Companies with simple-rules strategies must follow the rules religiously and avoid the temptation to change then too frequently. A consistent strategy helps managers sort through opportunities and gain short-term advantage by exploiting the attractive ones.

In stable markets, managers rely on complicated strategies built on detailed predictions of the future. But when business is complicated, strategy should be simple.

---

Since its founding in 1994, Yahoo! has emerged as one of the blue chips of the new economy. As the Internet's top portal, Yahoo! generates the astounding numbers we've come to expect from stars of the digital era—more than 100 million visits per day, annual sales growth approaching 200%, and a market capitalization that has exceeded the value of the Walt Disney Company. Yet Yahoo! also provides something we don't generally expect from Internet companies: profits.

Everyone recognizes the unprecedented success of Yahoo!, but it's not easily explained using traditional thinking about competitive strategy. Yahoo!'s rise can't

be attributed to an attractive industry structure, for
example. In fact, the Internet portal space is a strategist's
worst nightmare: it's characterized by intense rivalries,
instant imitators, and customers who refuse to pay a
cent. Worse yet, there are few barriers to entry. Nor is it
possible to attribute Yahoo!'s success to unique or valuable resources—its founders had little more than a computer and a great idea when they started the company.
As for strategy, many analysts would say it's not clear
that Yahoo! even has one. The company began as a catalog of Web sites, became a content aggregator, and eventually grew into a community of users. Lately it has
become a broad network of media, commerce, and communication services. If Yahoo! has a strategy, it would be
very hard to pin down using traditional, textbook
notions.

While the Yahoo! story is dramatic, it's far from
unique. Many other leaders of the new economy, including eBay and America Online, also rose to prominence by
pursuing constantly evolving strategies in market spaces
that were considered
unattractive according to traditional measures. And it's
not exclusively a new-
economy phenomenon. Com-
panies in even the oldest sectors of the economy have
excelled without the advantages of superior resources or
strategic positions. Consider Enron and AES in energy,
Ispat International in steel, Cemex in cement, and Voda-
fone and Global Crossing in telecommunications.

*The new economy's
most profound strategic
implication is that
companies must capture
unanticipated, fleeting
opportunities in
order to succeed.*

The performance of all these companies—despite
unattractive industry structures, few apparent resource

advantages, and constantly evolving strategies—raises critical questions. How did they succeed? More generally, what are the sources of competitive advantage in high-velocity markets? What does strategy mean in the new economy?

The secret of companies like Yahoo! is *strategy as simple rules*. Managers of such companies know that the greatest opportunities for competitive advantage lie in market confusion, so they jump into chaotic markets, probe for opportunities, build on successful forays, and shift flexibly among opportunities as circumstances dictate. But they recognize the need for a few key strategic processes and a few simple rules to guide them through the chaos. As one Internet executive explained: "I have a thousand opportunities a day; strategy is deciding which 50 to do." In traditional strategy, advantage comes from exploiting resources or stable market positions. In strategy as simple rules, by contrast, advantage comes from successfully seizing fleeting opportunities.

It's not surprising that a young company like Yahoo! should rely on strategy as simple rules. Entrepreneurs have always used that kind of opportunity-grabbing approach because it can help them win against established competitors. What is surprising is that strategy as simple rules makes sense for all kinds of companies— large and small, old and young—in fast-moving markets like those in the new economy. That's because, while information economics and network effects are important, the new economy's most profound strategic implication is that companies must capture unanticipated, fleeting opportunities in order to succeed.

Of course, theory is one thing, but putting it into practice is another. In fact, our recommendations reverse some prescriptions of traditional strategy. Rather than picking a position or leveraging a competence, managers should select a few key strategic processes. Rather than responding to a complicated world with elaborate strategies, they should craft a handful of simple rules. Rather than avoiding uncertainty, they should jump in.

## Zeroing in on Key Processes

Companies that rely on strategy as simple rules are often accused of lacking strategies altogether. Critics have derided AOL as "the cockroach of the Internet" for scurrying from one opportunity to the next. Some analysts accuse Enron of doing the same thing. From the outside, companies like these certainly appear to be following an "if it works, anything goes" approach. But that couldn't be further from the truth. Each company follows a disciplined strategy—otherwise, it would be paralyzed by chaos. And, as with all effective strategies, the strategy is unique to the company. But a simple-rules strategy and its underlying logic of pursuing opportunities are harder to see than traditional approaches. (The exhibit "Three Approaches to Strategy" compares the strategies of position, resources, and simple rules.)

Managers using this strategy pick a small number of strategically significant processes and craft a few simple rules to guide them. The key strategic processes should place the company where the flow of opportunities is swiftest and deepest. The processes might include product innovation, partnering, spinout creation, or new-market entry. For some companies, the choices are obvious—Sun Microsystems' focus on developing new products is a good example. For other companies, the selection of key processes might require some creativity—Akamai, for instance, has developed a focus on

# Three Approaches to Strategy

*Managers competing in business can choose among three distinct ways to fight. They can build a fortress and defend it; they can nurture and leverage unique resources; or they can flexibly pursue fleeting opportunities within simple rules. Each approach requires different skill sets and works best under different circumstances.*

| | Position | Resources | Simple Rules |
|---|---|---|---|
| **Strategic logic** | Establish position | Leverage resources | Pursue opportunities |
| **Strategic steps** | • Identify an attractive market<br>• Locate a defensible position<br>• Fortify and defend | • Establish a vision<br>• Build resources<br>• Leverage across markets | • Jump into the confusion<br>• Keep moving<br>• Seize opportunities<br>• Finish strong |
| **Strategic question** | Where should we be? | What should we be? | How should we proceed? |
| **Source of advantage** | Unique, valuable position with tightly integrated activity system | Unique, valuable, inimitable resources | Key processes and unique simple rules |
| **Works best in** | Slowly changing, well-structured markets | Moderately changing, well-structured markets | Rapidly changing, ambiguous markets |
| **Duration of advantage** | Sustained | Sustained | Unpredictable |
| **Risk** | It will be too difficult to alter position as conditions change | Company will be too slow to build new resources as conditions change | Managers will be too tentative in executing on promising opportunities |
| **Performance goal** | Profitability | Long-term dominance | Growth |

customer care. The simple rules provide the guidelines within which managers can pursue opportunities. Strategy, then, consists of the unique set of strategically significant processes and the handful of simple rules that guide them.

Autodesk, the global leader in software for design professionals, illustrates strategy as simple rules. In the mid-1990s, Autodesk's markets were mature, and the company dominated all of them. As a result, growth slowed to single-digit rates. CEO Carol Bartz was sure that her most-promising opportunities lay in making use of those Autodesk technologies—in areas such as wireless communications, the Internet, imaging, and global positioning—that hadn't yet been exploited. But she wasn't sure which new technologies and related products would be big winners. So she refocused the strategy on the product innovation process and introduced a simple, radical rule: the new-product development schedule would be shortened from a leisurely 18 to 24 months to, in some cases, a hyperkinetic three months. That changed the pace, scale, and strategic logic with which Autodesk tackled technology opportunities.

While a strategy of accelerating product innovation helped identify opportunities more quickly, Bartz lacked the cash to commercialize all of Autodesk's promising technologies. So she added a significant new strategy: spinouts. The first spinout, Buzzsaw.com, debuted in 1999. It allowed engineers to purchase construction materials using B2B exchange technology. Buzzsaw.com attracted significant venture capital and benefited from Autodesk's powerful brand and its customer relationships. Autodesk has since created a second spinout, RedSpark, and has developed simple rules for the new key process of spinning off companies.

A company's particular combination of opportunities and constraints often dictates the processes it chooses. Cisco, Autodesk, Lego, and Yahoo! began with strategies in which product innovation was dominant, but their emphases diverged. Cisco's new opportunities lay in the many new networking technologies that were emerging, but the company lacked the time and engineering talent to develop them all. In contrast to technology-rich and stock-price-poor Autodesk, which focused on spinouts, Cisco—with high market capitalization—found that acquisitions was the way to go. Despite its stratospheric market cap, Yahoo! went in yet another direction. The company wanted to exploit content and commerce opportunities but needed a lot of partners. Many were too big to acquire, so it created partnerships. Lego's best opportunities were in extending its power brand and philosophy into new markets. But since the company faced less competition and operated at a slower pace than Autodesk, Cisco, or Yahoo!, managers could grow organically into new product markets such as children's robotics, clothing, theme parks, and software.

## Simple Rules for Unpredictable Markets

Most managers quickly grasp the concept of focusing on key strategic processes that will position their companies where the flow of opportunities is most promising. But because they equate processes with detailed routines, they often miss the notion of simple rules. Yet simple rules are essential. They poise the company on what's termed in complexity theory "the edge of chaos," providing just enough structure to allow it to capture the best opportunities. It may sound counterintuitive, but the complicated improvisational movements that companies like AOL and Enron make as they pursue fleeting opportunities arise from simple rules.

Yahoo!'s managers initially focused their strategy on the branding and product innovation processes and lived by four product innovation rules: know the priority rank of each product in development, ensure that every engineer can work on every project, maintain the Yahoo! look in the user interface, and launch products quietly. As long as they followed the rules, developers could change products in any way they chose, come to work at any hour, wear anything, and bring along their dogs and significant others. One developer decided at midnight to build a new sports page covering the European soccer champion-ships. Within 48 hours, it became Yahoo!'s most popular page, with more than 100,000 hits per day. Since he knew which lines he had to stay within, he was free to run with a great idea when it occurred to him. A day later, he was back on his primary project. On a bigger scale, the simple rules, in particular the requirement that every engineer be able to work on every project, allowed Yahoo! to change 50% of the code for the enormously successful My Yahoo! service four weeks before launch to adjust to the changing market.[1]

Over the course of studying dozens of companies in turbulent and unpredictable markets, we've discovered that the simple rules fall into five broad categories. (See the exhibit "Simple Rules, Summarized.")

## HOW-TO RULES

Yahoo!'s how-to rules kept managers just organized enough to seize opportunities. Enron provides another how-to example. Its commodities-trading business focuses strategy on the risk management process with

## Simple Rules, Summarized

*In turbulent markets, managers should flexibly seize opportunities—but flexibility must be disciplined. Smart companies focus on key processes and simple rules. Different types of rules help executives manage different aspects of seizing opportunities.*

| Type | Purpose | Example |
| --- | --- | --- |
| How-to rules | They spell out key features of how a process is executed—"What makes our process unique?" | Akamai's rules for the customer service process: staff must consist of technical gurus, every question must be answered on the first call or e-mail, and R&D staff must rotate through customer service. |
| Boundary rules | They focus managers on which opportunities can be pursued and which are outside the pale. | Cisco's early acquisitions rule: companies to be acquired must have no more than 75 employees, 75% of whom are engineers. |
| Priority rules | They help managers rank the accepted opportunities. | Intel's rule for allocating manufacturing capacity: allocation is based on a product's gross margin. |
| Timing rules | They synchronize managers with the pace of emerging opportunities and other parts of the company. | Nortel's rules for product development: project teams must know when a product has to be delivered to the leading customer to win, and product development time must be less than 18 months. |
| Exit rules | They help managers decide when to pull out of yesterday's opportunities. | Oticon's rule for pulling the plug on projects in development: if a key team member—manager or not—chooses to leave the project for another within the company, the project is killed. |

two rules: each trade must be offset by another trade that allows the company to hedge its risk, and every trader must complete a daily profit-and-loss statement. Computer giant Dell focuses on the process of rapid reorganization (or patching) around focused customer segments. A key how-to rule for this process is that a business must be split in two when its revenue hits $1 billion.

## BOUNDARY RULES

Sometimes simple rules delineate boundary conditions that help managers sort through many opportunities quickly. The rules might center on customers, geography, or technologies. For example, when Cisco first moved to an acquisitions-led strategy, its boundary rule was that it could acquire companies with at most 75 employees, 75% of whom were engineers. At a major pharmaceutical company, strategy centers on the drug discovery process and several boundary rules: researchers can work on any of ten molecules (no more than four at once) specified by a senior research committee, and a research project must pass a few continuation hurdles related to progress in clinical trials. Within those boundaries, researchers are free to pursue whatever looks promising. The result has been a drug pipeline that's the envy of the industry.

Miramax—well known for artistically innovative movies such as *The Crying Game, Life is Beautiful*, and *Pulp Fiction*—has boundary rules that guide the all-important movie-picking process: first, every movie must revolve around a central human condition, such as love (*The Crying Game*) or envy (*The Talented Mr. Ripley*). Second, a movie's main character must be appealing but deeply flawed—the hero of *Shakespeare in Love* is gifted and charming but steals ideas from friends and betrays his wife. Third, movies must have a very clear story line with a beginning, middle, and end (although in *Pulp Fiction* the end comes first). Finally, there is a firm cap on production costs. Within the rules, there is flexibility to move quickly when a writer or director shows up with a great script. The result is an enormously creative and even surprising flow of movies and enough discipline to produce superior, consistent financial results. *The English Patient*, for example, cost $27 million to make, grossed more than $200 million, and grabbed nine Oscars.

Lego provides another illustration of boundary rules. At Lego, the product market-entry process is a strategic focus because of the many opportunities to extend the Lego brand and philosophy. But while there is plenty of flexibility, not every market makes the cut. Lego has a checklist of rules. Does the proposed product have the Lego look? Will children learn while having fun? Will parents approve? Does the product maintain high quality standards? Does it stimulate creativity? If an opportunity falls short on one hurdle, the business team can proceed, but ultimately the hurdle must be cleared. Lego children's wear, for example, met all the criteria except one: it didn't stimulate creativity. As a result, the members of the children's wear team worked until they figured out the answer—a line of mix-and-match clothing items that encouraged children to create their own fashion statements.

## PRIORITY RULES

Simple rules can set priorities for resource allocation among competing opportunities. Intel realized a long time ago that it needed to allocate manufacturing capacity among its products very carefully, given the enormous costs of fabrication facilities. At a time of extreme price volatility in the mid-1980s, when Asian chip manufacturers were disrupting world markets with severe price cuts and accelerated technological improvement, Intel followed a simple rule: allocate manufacturing capacity based on a product's gross margin. Without this rule, the company might have continued to allocate too much capacity to its traditional core memory business rather than seizing the opportunity to dominate the nascent and highly profitable microprocessor niche.[2]

## TIMING RULES

Many companies have timing rules that set the rhythm of key strategic processes. In fact, pacing is one of the important elements that set simple-rules strategies apart from traditional strategies. Timing rules can help synchronize a company with emerging opportunities and coordinate the company's various parts to capture them. Nortel Networks now relies on two timing rules for its strategically important product innovation process: project teams must always know

*Thick manuals of rules can be paralyzing. They can keep managers from seeing opportunities and moving quickly enough to capture them.*

when a product has to be delivered to the leading customer to win, and product development time must be less than 18 months. The first rule keeps Nortel in sync with cutting-edge customers, who represent the best opportunities. The second forces Nortel to move quickly into new opportunities while synchronizing the various parts of the corporation to do so. Together, the rules helped the company shift focus from perfecting its current products to exploiting market openings—to "go from perfection to hitting market windows," as CEO John Roth puts it. At an Internet-based service company where we worked, globalization was the process that put the company squarely in the path of superior opportunities. Managers drove new-country expansion at the rate of one new country every two months, thus maintaining constant movement into new opportunities. Many top Silicon Valley companies set timing rules for the length of the product innovation process. When developers approach a deadline, they drop features to meet the schedule. Such rhythms maintain movement and ensure that the market and various groups within the organization—from manufacturing to marketing to engineering—are on the same beat.

### EXIT RULES

Exit rules help managers pull out from yesterday's opportunities. At the Danish hearing-aid company Oticon, executives pull the plug on a product in development if a key team member leaves for another project. Similarly, at a major high-tech multinational where creating new businesses is a key strategic process, senior executives stop new initiatives that don't meet certain sales and profit goals within two years. (For a look at the flip side of simple rules, see "What Simple Rules Are Not" at the end of this article.)

## The Number of Rules Matters

Obviously, it's crucial to write the right rules. But it's also important to have the optimal number of rules. Thick manuals of rules can be paralyzing. They can keep managers from seeing opportunities and moving quickly enough to capture them. We worked with a computer maker, for example, whose minutely structured process for product innovation was highly efficient but left the company no flexibility to respond to market changes. On the other hand, too few rules can also paralyze. Managers chase too many opportunities or become confused about which to pursue and which to ignore. We worked with a biotech company that lagged behind the competition in forming successful partnerships, a key strategic process in that industry. Because the company lacked guidelines, development managers brought in deal after deal, and key scientists were pulled from clinical trials over and over again to perform due diligence. Senior management ended up rejecting most of the proposals. Executives may have had implicit rules, but nobody knew what they were. One business development manager lamented: "It would be so liberating if only I had a few guidelines about what I'm supposed to be looking for."

While creating the right number of rules—it's usually somewhere between two and seven—is central, companies arrive at the optimal number from different directions. On the one hand, young companies usually have too few rules, which prevents them from executing innovative ideas effectively. They need more structure, and they often have to build their simple rules from the ground up. On the other hand, older companies usually have too many rules, which keep them from competing effectively in turbulent markets. They need to throw out massively complex procedures and start over with a few easy-to-follow directives.

*While it's appealing to think that simple rules arise from clever thinking, they rarely do. More often, they grow out of experience, especially mistakes.*

The optimal number of rules for a particular company can also shift over time, depending on the nature of the business opportunities. In a period of predictability and focused opportunities, a company should have more rules in order to increase efficiency. When the landscape becomes less predictable and the opportunities more diffuse, it makes sense to have fewer rules in order to increase flexibility. When Cisco started to acquire aggressively, the "75 people, 75% engineers" rule worked extremely well—it ensured a match with Cisco's entrepreneurial culture and left the company with lots of space to maneuver. As the company developed more clarity and focus in its home market, Cisco recognized the need for a few more rules: a target must share Cisco's vision of where the industry is headed, it must have potential for short-term wins with current products, it must have potential for long-term wins with the follow-on product generation, it must have geographic proximity to Cisco, and its culture must be compatible with Cisco's. If a potential acquisition meets all five criteria, it gets a green light. If it meets four, it gets a yellow light—further consideration is required. A candidate that meets fewer than four gets a red light. CEO John Chambers believes that observing these simple rules has helped Cisco resist the temptation to make inappropriate acquisitions. More recently, Cisco has relaxed its rules (especially on proximity) to accommodate new opportunities as the company moves further afield into new technologies and toward new customers.

## How Rules Are Created

We're often asked where simple rules come from. While it's appealing to think that they arise from clever thinking, they rarely do. More often, they grow out of experience, especially mistakes. Take Yahoo! and its partnership-creation rules. An exclusive joint venture with a major credit card company proved calamitous. The deal locked Yahoo! into a relationship with a particular firm, thereby limiting e-commerce opportunities. After an expensive exit, Yahoo! developed two simple rules for partnership creation: deals can't be exclusive, and the basic service is always free.

At young companies, where there is no history to learn from, senior executives use experience gained at other companies. CEO George Conrades of Akamai, for example, drew on his decades of marketing experience to focus his company on customer service—a surprising choice of strategy for a high-tech venture. He then declared some simple rules: the company must staff the customer service group with technical gurus, every question must be answered on the first call or e-mail, and R&D people must rotate through customer care. These how-to rules shaped customer service at Akamai but left plenty of room for employees to innovate with individual customers.

Most often, a rough outline of simple rules already exists in some implicit form. It takes an observant manager to make them explicit and then extend them as business opportunities evolve. (It's even possible to trace a young company's evolution by examining how its simple rules have been applied over time.) EBay, for example, started out with two strong values: egalitarianism and community—or, as one user put it, "capitalism for the rest of us." Over time, founder and chairman Pierre Omidyar and CEO Meg Whitman made those values explicit in simple rules that helped managers predict which opportunities would work for eBay. Egalitarianism evolved into two simple how-to rules for running auctions: the number of buyers and sellers must be balanced, and transactions must be as transparent as possible. The first rule equalizes the power of buyers and sellers but does not restrict who can participate, so the eBay site is open to everyone, from individual collectors to corporations (indeed, several major retailers now use eBay as a quiet channel for their merchandise). The second rule gives all participants equal access to as much information as possible. This rule guided eBay managers into a series of moves such as creating feedback ratings on sellers, on-line galleries for expensive items, and authentication services from Lloyd's of London.

The business meaning of community was crystallized into a few simple rules, too: product ads aren't allowed (they compete with the community), prices for basic services must not be raised (increases hurt small members), and eBay must uphold high safety standards (a community needs to feel safe). The rules further clarified which opportunities made sense. For instance, it was okay to launch the PowerSellers program, which offers extra services for community members who sell frequently. It was also okay to allow advertising by financial services companies and to expand into Europe, because neither move broke the rules or threatened the community. On the other hand, it was not okay to have advertising deals with companies such as CDnow whose merchandise competes with the community. Only later did the economic value of the rules become apparent: the strength of the eBay community posed a formidable entry barrier to competitors, while egalitarianism created a high level of trust and transparency among traders that effectively differentiated eBay from its competitors.

It's entirely possible for two companies to focus on the same key process yet develop radically different simple rules to govern it. Consider Ispat International and Cisco. In the last decade, Ispat has gone from running a single steel mill in Indonesia to being the fourth-largest steel company in the world by using a new-economy strategy in an old-economy business. Founder Lakshmi Mittal's strategy centers on the acquisition process. But Ispat's rules for acquisitions look a whole lot different from Cisco's for the same process.

Ispat's rules include buying established, state-owned companies that have problems. Cisco's rules limit its acquisitions to young, well-run, VC-backed companies. Ispat's rules don't include geographic restrictions, so managers search the globe—Mexico, Kazakhstan, Ireland—for ailing companies. At least initially, Cisco's rules required exactly the opposite focus—the company stayed close to home with lots of acquisitions in Silicon Valley. Ispat focuses narrowly on two process technologies—DRI and electric arc furnaces—to drive companywide consistency. At Cisco, the whole point is to acquire new technologies. Ispat's rules center on finding companies in which costs can be cut from current operations. Cisco's rules gauge revenue gains from future products. The bottom line: same strategic process, same entrepreneurial emphasis on seizing fleeting opportunities, same superior wealth creation—but with totally different simple rules.

## Knowing When to Change

It's important for companies with simple-rules strategies to follow the rules religiously—think Ten Commandments, not optional suggestions—to avoid the temptation to change them too frequently. A consistent strategy helps managers rapidly sort through all kinds of opportunities and gain short-term advantage by exploiting the attractive ones. More subtly, it can lead to patterns that build long-term advantage, such as Lego's powerful brand position and Cisco's interrelated networking technologies.

Although it's unwise to churn the rules, strategies do go stale. Shifting the rules can sometimes rejuvenate strategy, but if the problems are deep, switching strategic processes may be necessary. The ability to switch to new strategic processes has been a success secret of the best new-economy companies. For example, Inktomi, a leader in Internet infrastructure software, augmented its original strategic focus on the product innovation process with a focus on the market entry process and a few boundary rules: the company must never produce a hardware product, never interface directly with end users, and always develop software for applications with many users and transactions (this exploits Inktomi's basic technology). Company managers did not restrict the business or revenue models. The result was successful new businesses in, for example, search engines, caching, and e-commerce engines. In fact, the company's second business, caching, is now its key growth driver. But CEO Dave Peterschmidt and his team have recently turned their attention to the sales process because corporations—a much bigger customer set than was available in their original portal market—are buying Inktomi software to manage intranets, thus opening a massive stream of new opportunities. Inktomi is turning to this new opportunity flow and crafting fresh simple rules. Inktomi is thus accelerating growth by adding new processes before old ones falter. If managers wait until the opportunity flow dries up before shifting processes, it's already too late. (For more details on the use of simple rules over time, see "Enron: Simple Rules and Opportunity Logic" at the end of this article.)

## What Is Strategy?

Like all effective strategies, strategy as simple rules is about being different. But that difference does not arise from tightly linked activity systems or leveraged core competencies, as in traditional strategies. It arises from focusing on key strategic processes and developing simple rules that shape those processes. When a pattern emerges from the processes—a pattern that creates network effects or economies of scale or scope—the result can be a long-term competitive advantage like the ones Intel and Microsoft achieved for over a decade. More often, the competitive advantage is short term.

The more significant point, though, is that no one can predict how long an advantage will last. An executive must manage, therefore, as if it could all end tomorrow. The new economy and other chaotic markets are too uncertain to do otherwise. From newcomers like Yahoo! founder Jerry Yang, who claims, "We live on the edge," to Dell's Michael Dell, who famously said, "The only constant is change," there's almost universal recognition that the most salient feature of competitive advantage in these markets is not sustainability but unpredictability.

In stable markets, managers can rely on complicated strategies built on detailed predictions of the future. But in complicated, fast-moving markets where significant growth and wealth creation can occur, unpredictability reigns. It makes sense to follow the lead of entrepreneurs and underdogs—seize opportunities in the here and now with a handful of rules and a few key processes. In other words, when business becomes complicated, strategy should be simple.

---

## What Simple Rules Are Not

IT IS IMPOSSIBLE TO DICTATE exactly what a company's simple rules should be. It is possible, however, to say what they should *not* be.

### Broad

Managers often confuse a company's guiding principles with simple rules. The celebrated "HP way," for example, consists of principles like "we focus on a high level of achievement and contribution" and "we encourage flexibility and innovation." The principles are designed to apply to every activity within the company, from purchasing to product innovation. They may create a productive culture, but they provide little concrete guidance for employees trying to evaluate a partner or decide whether to enter a new market. The most effective simple rules, in contrast, are tailored to a single process.

### Vague

Some rules cover a single process but are too vague to provide real guidance. One Western bank operating in Russia, for example, provided the following guideline for screening investment proposals: all investments must be currently undervalued and have potential for long-term capital appreciation. Imagine the plight of a newly hired associate who turns to that rule for guidance!

A simple screen can help managers test whether their rules are too vague. Ask: could any reasonable person argue the exact opposite of the rule? In the case of the bank in Russia, it is hard to imagine anyone suggesting that the company target overvalued companies with no potential for long-term capital appreciation. If your rules flunk this test, they are not effective.

## Mindless

Companies whose simple rules have remained implicit may find upon examining them that these rules destroy rather than create value. In one company, managers listed their recent partnership relationships and then tried to figure out what rules could have produced the list. To their chagrin, they found that one rule seemed to be: always form partnerships with small, weak companies that we can control. Another was: always form partnerships with companies that are not as successful as they once were. Again, use a simple test—reverse-engineer your processes to determine your implicit simple rules. Throw out the ones that are embarrassing.

## Stale

In high-velocity markets, rules can linger beyond their sell-by dates. Consider Banc One. The Columbus, Ohio-based bank grew to be the seventh-largest bank in the United States by acquiring more than 100 regional banks. Banc One's acquisitions followed a set of simple rules that were based on experience: Banc One must never pay so much that earnings are diluted, it must only buy successful banks with established management teams, it must never acquire a bank with assets greater than one-third of Banc One's, and it must allow acquired banks to run as autonomous affiliates. The rules worked well until others in the banking industry consolidated operations to lower their costs substantially. Then Banc One's loose confederation of banks was burdened with redundant operations, and it got clobbered by efficient competitors.

How do you figure out if your rules are stale? Slowing growth is a good indicator. Stock price is even better. Investors obsess about the future, while your own financials report the past. So if your share price is dropping relative to your competitors' share prices, or if your percentage of the industry's market value is declining, or if growth is slipping, your rules may need a refresh.

---

# Enron: Simple Rules and Opportunity Logic

SIMPLE RULES ESTABLISH a strategic frame—not a step-by-step recipe—to help managers seize fleeting opportunities. Few companies have followed the logic of opportunity or the discipline of simple rules as consistently as Enron. Fifteen years ago, the company's main line of business was interstate gas transmission—hardly a market space teeming with opportunities. Today, Enron makes markets in commodities ranging from pulp and paper to pollution-emission allowances. It also controls an expansive fiber-optic network, and runs an on-line exchange—EnronOnline—whose daily trading volume ranks it among the largest e-commerce sites.

Enron began its remarkable transformation by embracing uncertainty. While conventional wisdom dictates that managers avoid uncertainty, the logic of opportunity dictates that they seek it out. Like the outlaw Willie

Sutton, who robbed banks because that's where the money was, Enron managers embraced uncertainty because that's where the juicy opportunities lay. Enron's managers expanded from their traditional pipeline business into wholesale energy distribution, trading, and global energy. At a time when other energy executives were doggedly defending their regulatory protection, Enron CEO Ken Lay aggressively lobbied to accelerate deregulation in order to create new opportunities for Enron to exploit.

Once they had plunged into the brave new world of deregulated energy, Enron managers faced a challenge common to new-economy companies but rare among utilities—how to navigate among the overabundance of opportunities. To shift among opportunities, Enron mostly relied on small moves, which are faster and safer than large ones. Often, the moves were made from the bottom—many of Enron's new trading businesses began as one-person operations.

The company needed to provide some structure for all this movement among opportunities. Enter key processes and simple rules. In Enron's commodities-trading businesses, for example, strategy centers on the risk management process and two simple rules: all trades must be balanced with an offsetting trade to minimize unhedged risk, and each trader must report a daily profit-and-loss statement. As long as they follow these how-to rules, Enron's traders are free to pursue new opportunities. The strategy has led the company to pioneer markets for commodities that had never been traded before, including fiber-optic bandwidth, pollution-emission credits, and weather derivatives—contracts that allow companies to hedge their weather-related risk.

When it comes to strategic processes and simple rules, one size doesn't fit all. When Enron pioneered outsourced energy-management services in 1996, every organization with a high energy bill was a potential customer. To select from the overwhelming number of opportunities, Enron managers focused on the customer-screening process and articulated a few boundary rules to identify attractive customers: a target customer must have outsourced before, energy must not be the core of its business, and contacts with Enron must already exist somewhere within the company. In addition, Enron's salespeople must deal directly with the CEO or CFO, because only the top executives can assess the potential for companywide savings and then commit. In four years, Enron Energy Services has grown from nothing to $15 billion in sales.

When pursuing novel opportunities such as trading weather derivatives and providing outsourced energy management, it's impossible for Enron managers to predict which initiatives will take off. Managers must be prepared, therefore, to reinforce successful moves that gain traction, even if those successes run counter to managers' preconceived notions of what should work. Fiber-optic cable, for example, had little to do with Enron's core energy business, but managers quickly recognized its potential and backed a winner.

In uncertain markets, not every opportunity pans out. Savvy managers respond not by making fewer moves but by cutting their losses quickly: after Enron's acquisition of Portland General failed to work out according to plan, the company quickly put the utility back on the block. Managers at Enron also try to build on mistakes by salvaging what did work and recombining it with other resources to create new opportunities. This recombination works particularly well for large companies like Enron that have an abundance of "genetic material"—technologies, products, and expertise—for creative combinations. So while the Portland General acquisition as a whole failed to pan out, Enron managers salvaged the utility's fledgling broadband cable business and combined it with Enron's expertise in trading to create a host of new opportunities in buying and selling broadband capacity and running a fiber-optic network.

The Enron story also illustrates the importance of "finishing strong" when managers discover a huge opportunity. In chaotic markets, the initial move, no matter how masterful, rarely yields unambiguous success. Rather, initial moves unearth subsequent opportunities that may prove huge, as e-commerce and broadband cable have for Enron. The key risks in pursuing uncertain opportunities are that moves may become too tentative—too prone to quick retreat—and that managers might grow overly cautious in pursuing the big opportunities that promise outsized payoffs. Enron has succeeded, in large part, because its managers finish strong. In broadband, the company reinforced early successes through moves such as delivering movies on demand in partnership with Blockbuster. Similarly, after Enron's initial foray into Internet trading took off, top executives rapidly redeployed resources from throughout the company to scale EnronOnline.

# Notes

1. Data on the Yahoo! product launch is drawn from Marco Iansiti and Alan MacCormack, "Living on Internet Time," HBS case no. 6-97-052, 1999.

2. Data on Intel's exit from microprocessors is drawn from Robert A. Burgelman, Dennis L. Carter, and Raymond S. Bamford, "Intel Corporation: The Evolution of an Adaptive Organization," Stanford Graduate School of Business case no. SM-65, 1999.

Originally published in January 2001
Reprint R0101G

# How Financial Engineering Can Advance Corporate Strategy

PETER TUFANO

## Executive Summary

PRACTITIONERS OF A NEW technical specialty—financial engineering—can help senior managers achieve their companies' objectives. Financial engineering can not only reduce the cost of existing activities but also make possible the development of new products, services, and markets. Peter Tufano presents five case studies that illustrate innovative applications of financial engineering and helps managers determine when such techniques are appropriate.

The cases highlight five companies that faced different challenges: Enron Capital & Trade Resources, Tennessee Valley Authority, Rhône-Poulenc, Cemex, and MW Petroleum Corporation. All of them found that traditional approaches were inadequate—the costs or the risks seemed too high. A nontraditional solution, however, required that the companies commit to bearing risks

123

that their customers, employees, or counterparties sought to shed. Without a means of structuring, valuing, and mitigating those risks, the initiatives that the companies pursued seemed doomed to failure. In the end, the innovative approach was made possible by the concepts, tools, and markets of financial engineers.

The cases show that collaboration between managers and financial engineers can help create a competitive edge by differentiation products through enhanced price and delivery options, by increasing production capacity with flexible alternatives to capital investment, by changing the risk characteristics of holding stock, or by keeping strategic mergers on track through the creation of win-win situations.

---

Lᴇᴀᴅᴇʀs ᴏꜰ ꜱᴜᴄᴄᴇꜱꜱꜰᴜʟ ʙᴜꜱɪɴᴇꜱꜱᴇꜱ build long-term relationships with customers, suppliers, employees, and shareholders. They make farsighted investments to support and develop their core competencies. They act quickly to ensure that short-term obstacles do not disrupt their long-term strategies. In conceiving and implementing corporate strategies, managers have always drawn on the skills of many specialists, from marketers to production experts. Now a small but growing number of senior managers have found that practitioners of a new technical specialty—financial engineering—can help them achieve their companies' strategic objectives. They have found that, like other technological breakthroughs such as cheap computing power, financial engineering has the potential not only to reduce the cost of existing activities but also to make possible the development of new products, services, and markets.

The notion that financial engineering—the use of derivatives to manage risk and create customized financial instruments—can advance a company's strategic goals might contradict the impression one gets from recent stories in the press. In many of these tales, traders within the finance staff use derivatives to speculate on the steepness of the yield curve or on movements of exchange rates. It appears that these bets have not been driven by the company's business strategy and that senior managers have been unaware of choices made deep within their finance organizations. When misguided wagers backfire, companies lose millions and executives lose their jobs. Managers who seek to avoid disasters certainly must pay careful attention to these cautionary tales. Nevertheless, these accounts could easily give the impression that financial engineering is not used, and indeed should not be used, by nonfinancial companies to advance core business goals. That impression would be wrong.

*Managers need to keep abreast of their rivals' successful uses of financial engineering.*

It is well to recognize the pitfalls of new technologies, but failure to appreciate their true competitive value can be shortsighted and ultimately hazardous. Forward-looking managers need to keep abreast of their rivals' successful uses of promising breakthroughs like financial engineering. Unfortunately, those are the stories that remain untold. Were they to be told, managers would learn of leading organizations that have used financial engineering to solve classic and vexing business problems. These are not narrow finance problems that involve shaving a few basis points off financing costs or shedding transaction exposures arising from sales abroad. Rather, they are broad strategic problems—in marketing, production, human resources, investor relations, and strategic restructuring—for which advanced financial techniques have offered new solutions. This article presents five case studies that illustrate innovative applications of financial engineering and offers managers guidance for determining when such techniques are appropriate.

The cases highlight five corporations—three headquartered in the United States, one in France, and one in Mexico—that produce and market gas, electricity, chemicals, cement, or oil. Although the companies faced different management challenges, their goals were clear and their opportunities well defined. Traditional approaches toward achieving their objectives, however, seemed inadequate—either the costs or the risks appeared to be too high. The outline of a new, nontraditional solution was not hard to discern. But the innovative approach required that the companies commit themselves to bearing risks that their customers, employees, or counterparties sought to shed. Without a means of structuring, valuing, and mitigating those risks, the strategic initiatives that management pursued seemed doomed to failure. In the end, the innovative approach was made possible by the concepts, tools, and markets of financial engineers.

The cases demonstrate that close collaboration between general managers and financial engineers can help create a competitive edge in a variety of ways: *How can a producer of a commodity like natural gas differentiate its product?* by differentiating products through enhanced price and delivery options, by increasing production capacity with flexible alternatives to capital investment, by changing the risk characteristics of holding stock, or by keeping strategic mergers on track through the creation of win-win situations. The underlying aim of the cases is to follow the eye of the financial engineer who thinks like a strategist (or the strategist who thinks like a financial engineer). That means "following the risk" through the process of identifying the sources of risk, evaluating the strategic advantage of bearing risk, creating financial instruments to transfer risk, and using financial markets to value and shed risk.

# Controlling Volatility: Enron Capital & Trade Resources

Producers and distributors of regulated commodity products, such as natural gas or electricity, have not generally been known for their sophisticated marketing programs. Before deregulation, there was little need or incentive to differentiate their products. But price decontrols, open distribution systems, and market economics have changed all that. How, then, can a commodity producer succeed in a competitive environment? Elementary strategy suggests that the company must either be the lowest-cost provider or distinguish its product from the competition. And yet it would seem almost senseless for a company to establish a brand name for a product like methane, which can be fully described as one molecule of carbon attached to four molecules of hydrogen.

This was the challenge confronting Enron Capital & Trade Resources (ECT), a subsidiary of Enron Corporation of Houston, Texas—a diversified natural gas company that explores for and produces gas, operates pipelines, and builds and operates power plants around the world. ECT's recent success in the natural gas business can be attributed in part to its ability to create a line of product and service options by using financial engineering. As Jeffrey K. Skilling, chairman and CEO of ECT, puts it, "Selling natural gas is getting to be a real business, like selling washing machines. We're taking the simplest commodity there is, a methane molecule, and we're packaging and delivering it under a brand name, the way General Electric does."

ECT's managers had learned from a decade of instability in the natural gas market that their product was about more than carbon and hydrogen and that users of natural gas cared very much about such characteristics as reliable delivery and predictable prices. From 1938 to 1978, the price of natural gas had been under regulatory control, and buyers and sellers had known that prices would be fairly predictable. In the early 1970s, price controls together with the oil embargo in the Middle East led to severe gas shortages and precipitated the industry's deregulation from the wellhead to the end user. A series of legal rulings and market developments abrogated the standard industry contracts, which presold fixed quantities of gas at fixed prices. By 1990, more than three-fourths of all gas sales were at spot prices. Natural gas prices were more volatile than oil prices and, on occasion, four times as volatile as the Standard & Poor's 500 index.

In the late 1980s, ECT's managers sensed a market opportunity. Their vision was to create a "gas bank" that would serve as an intermediary between buyers and sellers, allowing both to shed their unwanted risks. Focusing on buyers, ECT's marketers reasoned that bundling methane molecules, reliable delivery, and predictable prices into a single package would define a clear product line and communicate the company's unique skills.

Further, by giving the package a distinctive name, they could perform the seemingly impossible trick of creating a brand name for methane.

Accordingly, ECT developed a family of products called EnFolio Gas Resource Agreements—gas-supply contracts that could be customized according to the quantity, time period, price index, and settlement terms specified. One local gas utility could buy EnFolio Gas-Bank and be assured of a fixed volume at a fixed price. Another might prefer EnFolio Index, which offered a fixed volume at a price tied to a natural gas index. A third might choose EnFolio GasCap, which delivered a fixed volume at a price tied to a natural gas index and capped at a previously determined level. Given the range of variables, each product could be sold under a nearly infinite set of specific conditions. ECT's marketing strategy, which stressed the company's ability to help gas consumers avoid unpredictable prices, included an amusing advertising campaign that featured a large black dot called Spot, representing the spot price of gas. In one ad, Spot was in a hospital bed. An erratic chart tracked its vital signs, and the caption read, "See Spot. See Spot having problems long-term."

ECT's crucial insight was that the extraordinary volatility of natural gas prices and the fluctuations in supply offered the company the opportunity to distinguish its product and to profit by managing the risks of uncertainty experienced by gas producers and consumers. Buyers and sellers would, in effect, pass their risk on to ECT. But ECT realized that it would have to manage the gas bank's long-term contracts carefully to avoid falling into the trap that had plagued the savings and loan industry, in which fixed-rate, long-term mortgages were funded by short-term interest rates paid to depositors. That mismatch of assets and liabilities had nearly bankrupted an entire industry when interest rates rose. ECT's risk managers have clear instructions to develop a hedging strategy that minimizes net gas exposures, and the company has invested millions of dollars in hardware, software, and hundreds of highly trained personnel to eliminate mismatches and ensure that fluctuations in gas prices do not jeopardize the company's existence.

Understanding customers' needs and developing a supporting marketing strategy did not require any knowledge of financial engineering. But creating the contracts and ensuring that the company did not expose itself to excessive risks were classic exercises in financial engineering. ECT's success—measured by both market share and profits—illustrates how financial engineers, working with marketers and strategists, can differentiate a commodity product without taking on undue risk.

## Adding Capacity with Virtual Bricks and Mortar: TVA

Senior managers facing projections of increased demand have to confront difficult decisions about whether to make or buy production capacity to meet that demand. The problem can be particularly vexing when building new capacity entails large-scale capital financing that may limit precious flexibility in a rapidly changing market. Costly production assets with projected useful lives of several decades could be rendered obsolete almost overnight. For the managers of Tennessee Valley Authority, the problem was even more acute because government policy limited their ability to finance new projects, and their industry was in a period of unprecedented upheaval. How could TVA meet its customers' needs without exposing itself either to market uncertainties or to large investments?

Founded in 1933, TVA was set up by Congress to manage the waters of the Tennessee River to produce electricity for the southeastern United States. At first, TVA built hydroelectric dams, and in later years, coal-fired-steam and nuclear power plants. Throughout its history, TVA met the increased demand for power by turning to its engineers, who transformed bricks, mortar, turbines, and reactors into energy. By mid-1994, TVA's demand forecasts indicated that for all but its lowest projections, it would have to continue to add capacity; for its highest projections, additional peak capacity would be required as soon as 1997.

But building new capacity is not inexpensive. One estimate puts the cost of TVA's nuclear power program over its 28-year history at $25 billion. In mid-1994, the capital expenditures necessary for TVA to meet its forecasted demand by the year 2000 were projected to be about $1.7 billion per year for the next six years. Numbers like these were putting pressure on TVA's capital budget.

Two other factors complicated TVA's ability to meet increasing demand. First, by setting TVA's debt ceiling at $30 billion, Congress limited the company's ability to finance new projects. In 1994, TVA's debt already stood at $26 billion, and its own board had set an internal cap approximately 10% below that imposed by Congress. Second, the deregulation of the electric power industry had begun, and the electricity market was in a state of flux. In the new market for power, electricity could be bought and sold for spot or future delivery. In the United Kingdom, brokers of power already could trade primitive

futures contracts. In the western United States, the
Western Systems Power Pool operated as a power
exchange for its members. And the New York Mercantile
Exchange was actively discussing the specifications of an
exchange-traded futures contract on electric power. By
the end of 1994, 80 entities had applied to the Federal
Energy Regulatory Commission to become over-the-
counter brokers or marketers of power in what was
thought to be the beginning of one of the nation's biggest
emerging markets.

The evolving markets for power clearly offered TVA a
way to meet increasing demand by buying power rather
than making it with bricks and mortar. Buying long-term
fixed-price and fixed-quantity contracts might require a
smaller up-front capital investment than would building
new generating plants. But that strategy wouldn't necessarily solve the problem of uncertain demand—the question of when and how much to buy. TVA could vary the
amount of energy its power plants produced in a matter
of minutes; and because electricity is not easily stored,
that flexibility was a critical aspect of the business. Given
the volatility of prices in the emerging power markets,
flexibility was becoming even more important. Thus for
*buying* power to be an adequate substitute for *making*
power, it would have to give TVA the same flexibility
that the company's power plants could. It looked as
though long-term contracts that locked in fixed amounts
at fixed prices would not fit the bill.

In early 1994, members of the Customer Planning
Group at TVA, all engineers by training, began to discuss
a new idea. Why couldn't TVA purchase call options on
power that would give it the right, but not the obligation,
to buy power from other utilities? By purchasing call
options on electricity, TVA could buy additional power

as needed. The call options could create a virtual power plant for TVA that acted like the real options that the company had in its bricks-and-mortar plants. Just as TVA could decide the level *Concepts drawn from* at which to operate a par- *financial markets will help* ticular generating source— *TVA manage the risk* sometimes on a daily basis, *of an options portfolio.* based on market demand and prices—so it could choose whether to exercise its options to buy power. If the company's low energy forecasts were borne out, it might choose to buy less additional power, but if the demand for energy was strong, it could exercise all its options. Similarly, it could choose whether to exercise its options on the basis of prevailing energy prices.

A number of questions remained: How could TVA ensure that its power counterparties would perform both technically and financially on their contracts? How should the option contracts be structured? How would TVA evaluate and price the various contracts? Through the spring and summer of 1994, the TVA team hammered out the mechanism for soliciting market prices from potential sellers of options. In July 1994, it issued a request for proposal for option purchase agreements (OPAs), formally seeking quotations on electricity options. By December 1994, it had received 138 separate bids totaling nearly 22,000 megawatts of power. During the winter and spring of 1995, the team evaluated the proposals, created a shortlist, and began to negotiate with potential counterparties.

The insight that TVA needed flexibility in acquiring new capacity did not require any financial engineering skills, but the implementation of the option purchase plan did. Concepts borrowed from the financial markets will help TVA value its OPAs, compare them with the traditional alternative (building plants), and manage the risk of an options portfolio. The financial engineers who structure, value, and manage these portfolios of option contracts may someday prove to be as valuable to a utility's future as the engineers who design hydroelectric, coal, and nuclear power plants. Perhaps as important, the information that electric power markets will provide to both producers and consumers will allow managers to make better investment decisions, even about traditional bricks-and-mortar projects.

## Reducing Stockholders' Risks: Rhône-Poulenc and Cemex

When investors shy away from a stock, it is probably because they think that the risks of investment are too high relative to the likely return. The managers whose stocks are avoided, however, may believe that such judgments are unwarranted or ill informed. They may want to educate investors and communicate confidence in their company's stock, especially when the potential investors are their own employees. Many managers and scholars agree

*Rhône-Poulenc needed to reduce the risks of stock ownership for employees and avoid prohibitive risks of its own.*

that workers tend to be most productive when their financial interests are aligned with those of the company's shareholders. One way to achieve this community of interests and to motivate workers is to tie compensation to stock price performance through executive stock ownership or employee stock ownership plans. Although companies can, of course, give stock to employees, they obviously would prefer that employees purchase shares. But they may find it difficult to persuade them to buy, especially when the prevailing business culture has made workers risk averse and there is no tradition of employee stock ownership in any form.

That was the problem confronting officials of the French government and managers of Rhône-Poulenc, the leading French life sciences and chemical company. Rhône-Poulenc had been nationalized in 1982, but more than a decade later a new regime sought to return the organization to private ownership, and a massive equity offering was planned to sell shares to global investors. Government officials and Rhône-Poulenc managers, deeming that broad participation by employees was critical to the private entity's long-term success, were excited by the prospect of employees having a direct interest in the value of its stock. When, in early 1993, an initial block of Rhône-Poulenc shares was sold in a partial privatization, both the government and the company took measures to encourage employees to buy shares. The state granted employees a 10% discount off the market price of the shares, and Rhône-Poulenc sweetened the deal by giving them an extra 15% discount in addition to the right to pay for the stock over 12 months. Despite those incentives, the employees' response was disappointing: Only 20% chose to participate, and only three-fourths of the employee allotment was sold.

As full privatization approached in late 1993, managers of Rhône-Poulenc and their counterparts at the French Treasury considered even more aggressive traditional incentives, such as further discounts, free shares, and interest-free loans. These sweeteners, however, had two problems: First, they might prove very costly both to the government and to Rhône-Poulenc. Second, the

Treasury and the managers suspected that even these measures would be insufficient because they failed to address the employees' fundamental fear of holding stock—the fear of losing their entire investment. The managers and the government worried that employees, whose economic well-being was already largely dependent on Rhône-Poulenc, would not take on a greater stake in the company; they needed a solution that would reduce or eliminate the risks of stock ownership for employees *and* avoid prohibitive costs or risks to themselves. How could they meet both those goals?

This was another classic opportunity for financial engineering, and the company's financial advisers at Bankers Trust offered the following solution: Why not provide employees with a guaranteed minimum return on their investments, which could be paid for by forgoing a part of their interest in the stock if it appreciated? In simple terms, employees could be offered a stock investment in Rhône-Poulenc that gave them voting rights and guaranteed a minimum return of 25% over four and a half years plus two-thirds of the appreciation of the stock over its initial level. If the company performed poorly, employees would not suffer any loss, and if it did well, they would gain, although not as much as they would have had they held regular shares. Thus the agreement would address the employees' fear of losing their money, as was amply demonstrated by their overwhelming acceptance of the plan. The proposed guaranteed shares, described in information sessions and on videotapes, turned out to be a successful portion of Rhône-Poulenc's oversubscribed offering.

But what about the costs to Rhône-Poulenc and the French government? Neither wanted to bear the risk of the guarantees if share prices fell. Here, too, they turned to their financial intermediaries, who assumed responsibility for managing the risk of the employee portfolio in financial markets. The financial engineers who structured the deal and managed the portfolio profited from the transaction while attracting praise and new business with their novel proposal. More important, by using the tools of risk management, they supported a well-conceived human resources policy that was an integral part of the company's strategy. And, thanks to financial engineering, Rhône-Poulenc's innovative approach had a net cost that was no higher than it would have been had the company used any of the traditional sweeteners. Management's insight that guaranteeing a minimum return on employee stock ownership would alleviate workers' concerns did not require any special knowledge of finance. Nor did the rank and file have to understand that they were financing the purchase of a put option by selling calls. But the skills of financial engineers were essential to ensure that Rhône-Poulenc kept the promises it made to employees.

Rhône-Poulenc's need to communicate confidence in its stock highlights a common management concern. Virtually every manager at one time or another believes that his or her stock is undervalued. If a company is using its stock to acquire other companies or if executive compensation is based on stock-price appreciation, undervaluation may be especially troublesome. Consider the case of Cemex, the largest cement producer in the Americas and the second-largest industrial company in Mexico. In 1992, when Cemex announced its strategic acquisition of two Spanish cement manufacturers, its stock fell dramatically in response. The market undervaluation was both extreme and crippling. What could Cemex do to communicate its confidence to investors?

The managers' first line of defense, meeting with investors and analysts, apparently failed, and the second "normal" solution, a stock buyback, was complicated by Mexican law. Cemex's financial advisers at J.P. Morgan then suggested an alternative that would comply with Mexican law while achieving the same purpose as a buyback: Instead of *buying* its stock, Cemex could *sell* investors an option (the right but not the obligation) to sell their stock back at any time over the next year for a fixed price. In the financial engineers' terminology, Cemex could issue a put on its own stock. In effect, it would commit to buy back its shares, guaranteeing a minimum price to any investor who bought the put. Whereas companies sometimes quietly sell (or write) puts in conjunction with their stock-buyback programs, J.P. Morgan was recommending a well-publicized sale of puts to communicate Cemex's conviction that its share price was too low.

Cemex had publicly committed to bearing a large portion of its investors' risks, but there was one remaining problem: If the company's share price plummeted, Cemex would not have the resources to honor its guarantees. The company's advisers at J.P. Morgan, however, were willing to issue and back the securities, called equity buyback obligation rights (EBORs), themselves. The proposal was a classic example of financial engineering: The specialists could price the EBORs and manage their risks in the financial markets.

Cemex's puts were a close cousin of the guarantees that Rhône-Poulenc offered its employees and apparently were just as effective. Between the time of the board meeting at which the EBORs were discussed and the actual offering, the company's stock recovered nearly half of its earlier decline. It is impossible to tell whether the response was caused by the public signal sent by Cemex, the trust implied by J.P. Morgan's issuance of the securities, or unrelated movements in the stock's price. Regardless of the cause, financial engineering (in this case, the sale of puts) offered a viable alternative to communicating confidence in stock through press releases and straight buybacks.

# Bridging the Gap Between Buyer and Seller: MW Petroleum Corporation

For the thousands of mergers and acquisitions consummated in a given year, there are probably thousands more that never get completed. Although some of those deals fail because of big differences in the perceptions of buyer and seller, others fail even though the gaps between the two parties are quite small. Given the right technical resources, skilled negotiators often can find ways to close the gaps, removing impediments to the fulfillment of their company's strategic plans.

In early 1991, a proposed transaction that would help both Amoco Corporation and Apache Corporation achieve their strategic goals looked as if it might bust. Amoco, an integrated petroleum and chemical corporation with sales of more than $28 billion, had emerged from a long-term, multiyear strategic assessment of its business with the conclusion that, given the company's cost structure, it should dispose of marginal oil and gas properties. So it created a new organization, MW Petroleum Corporation, as a freestanding exploration and development entity with working interests in 9,500 wells in more than 300 producing fields. Among Amoco's options was the ability to sell MW Petroleum as a mid-size independent petroleum company. Amoco and its

financial adviser, Morgan Stanley Group, then marketed
MW Petroleum to potential international and domestic
buyers. Among them, Apache Corporation, an independent oil and gas company with revenues of $270 million,
showed the most serious interest. Apache was an aggressive acquirer of oil and gas properties whose strategy was
to acquire properties that majors like Amoco believed
were marginal and then use its expertise and low-cost
operations to achieve substantially higher profits.
According to Apache's chairman and CEO, Raymond
Plank, the strategy "is a bit like a pig following a cow
through the cornfield. The scraps are pretty good for
someone with our particular mission." The MW
Petroleum deal was an attractive set of scraps.

The sale of MW Petroleum to Apache looked like a
strategic win-win for both companies—if they could find
an acceptable price. In the spring of 1991, however, the
oil and gas markets had just passed through a tumul-
tuous period. Iraq's invasion of Kuwait had not only
pushed oil prices to historic highs but also increased
uncertainty about their direction. In this environment,
Amoco was bullish and Apache bearish about future oil
prices. So although Amoco and Apache agreed on most
of the technical characteristics of MW Petroleum, their
differences over oil prices set a roadblock to the deal.
More important, Apache's bankers, who would fund the
acquisition, were very conservative about future oil
prices and based their proposed loan on worst-case scenarios. With the gap between buyer and seller equaling
perhaps 10% of the transaction value, the deal appeared
to be dead. Strategic goals are fine, but only if they can be
accomplished at a reasonable price.

That might have been the end of the story—another
set of discussions derailed by a failure to agree, with nei-

ther party willing to take the risk of a compromise. In this case, however, the disagreement was about future commodity prices, not about the inherent characteristics of the business being bought and sold. Although both parties were committed to their forecasts, they eventually realized they could find common ground by sharing the risk of future oil price movements while at the same time addressing the concerns of the bankers financing the deal. The solution hinged on a remarkably simple piece of financial engineering.

Amoco, which was more optimistic about oil and gas prices, could write Apache a capped price-support guarantee. Under the guarantee, if oil prices fell below a designated "price support" level in the first two years after the sale, Amoco would make compensating payments to Apache. With this support in hand, Apache would see short-term revenues and profits bolstered were oil and gas prices to soften. In turn, its lenders would be assured of sufficient cash flow to make the required debt service. In return for the guarantee, Apache would pay Amoco if oil or gas prices exceeded a designated "price sharing" level over the next five to eight years. Although Apache would end up paying more for MW Petroleum if oil or gas prices rose, the corresponding rise in revenues would provide the means to make the payments. By forgoing some of the upside, Apache could insure itself against the downside. The agreement was a win-win solution because each party would get the price it had forecast if that forecast was right—so both parties felt that they got the better deal.

By the same token, either company might regret having structured the transaction as it did. Nevertheless, by using a simple piece of financial engineering, both could accomplish their strategic goals in an environment of great uncertainty about future commodity prices. They found a way of sharing risks that made the chief executives and boards of both companies comfortable with the transaction. It did not take financial engineering skills to recognize that the risks of this deal could be shared. Nor did the buyer and seller have to understand that they had created a *collar*—a combination of a call option and a put option. Financial engineers, however, could value the collar by using actual data and financial models. Moreover, their pricing exercise was not merely theoretical. After the deal was closed, both sides were approached to sell off their positions and thus had the choice of monetizing the options and closing their risk exposures.

*Business leaders in these five cases did not seek to take on risk for risk's sake but, rather, risk for strategy's sake.*

## Applying Financial Engineering

All the case studies presented here show how financial engineering can offer solutions to intractable problems. Although the cases differ in many respects, managers in each one recognized the need, for the sake of their own strategic goals, to help others bear risks. Financial engineers were then able to structure, value, and manage the transfer of those risks. Further similarities among the cases raise a number of questions that managers should consider when deciding whether it is appropriate to apply financial engineering techniques.

**Is your ability to commit to bearing additional risk critical to your strategic success?** The use of financial engineering in these five cases contrasts with traditional forms of risk management, in which financial managers, seemingly divorced from the rest of the organization, inherit a set of exposures and manage their risk. Business leaders in these five cases knowingly took on risks to satisfy their customers, employees, stockholders, or negotiation counterparties. They did not seek to take on risk for risk's sake but, rather, risk for strategy's sake. The anticipated value of their transactions would come primarily from the strategic gains made possible by them. Although ECT, for example, sold fixed-price gas contracts, its primary goal was not to gain when gas prices rose or fell but rather to profit over the long term by differentiating its product. Similarly, Rhône-Poulenc's primary purpose was not to profit from movements in its stock value but to benefit from the increased personal investment and productivity of its employees.

**Is there an existing or potential market for the kinds of risks you need to bear?** Financial engineers are experts in transforming the risk-and-return characteristics of investments, and they are assisted by deep markets with low transaction costs. The more closely they can correlate the risk they seek to modify to a traded market with established contract forms, the more likely they are to find a feasible solution. Some risks, such as a potential rise or fall in a broad stock index, are very common, and claims on these risks are actively traded in public and private markets. Other risks are more idiosyncratic. But even a risk as personal as the potential property loss due to an auto accident can be mitigated—not in a market but through the risk sharing of property insurance. Financial engineering has proved to be most useful in protecting against potential failures caused by or related to movements in financial or commodity markets—in the present cases, the stock markets for Rhône-Poulenc and Cemex, and the commodity markets for the others.

Financial markets offer the opportunity to exchange risks at reasonably low transaction costs. Managers and academics should recognize that an efficient market, being essentially a zero-sum game, makes it difficult if not impossible to profit by taking on fairly priced risks. And they should be skeptical about whether companies should assume those risks. But again, it should be remembered that the five companies used financial engineering, in large measure, to shed the risks they took on. To the extent that they accepted risk, the "profits" they sought were not in the financial markets but rather in the product "market" for reliable gas, the labor "market" for committed French employees, or the acquisition and divestiture "market" for marginal oil properties. In an important sense, the companies were arbitraging risks between efficient financial markets and less efficient nonfinancial markets.

What is remarkable about these companies is their willingness to pursue financial engineering even though the relevant markets they faced were not very deep or well developed. None of them could find a premade derivative contract at an exchange that would answer their needs. Yet the importance of their problems and the lack of traditional business solutions motivated them to construct tailor-made solutions. While these tailored solutions may have been expensive, they were less expensive and more effective than the alternatives.

**Can you structure a contract that transfers the risk at a reasonable price without forcing you to incur unacceptable risks?** Financial engineering, of course, is not free, and transactions that transfer risk characteristically require cash payments or entail other contingent risks owing to the nature of the transactions. Managers who use financial engineering must understand those costs or new risks.

Managers obviously need to consider the cash costs of selling risks. For example, the owner of a stock portfolio might pay cash for a put option that gives him or her the right to sell the portfolio for a fixed price at some future time, thereby setting a floor value on the stock-and-option package. Cemex's EBORs and TVA's proposed purchase of call options both involve such up-front cash payments. Furthermore, when companies use financial engineering to obtain flexibility, they should understand and allow for the additional cash costs they may incur if they later change their plans.

Often, the price of shedding risk is taking on another risk or giving up some of the upside potential of a future transaction or rate movement. That is how Apache, Rhône-Poulenc's employees, and the purchasers of EnFolio GasBank products protected themselves against adverse movements in the price of oil, stock, or gas. In these forms of risk barter, the terms of trade were explicit and understood by all parties, but the allegations surrounding some recent cases of leveraged swaps underscore the need to make such understandings very clear.

In addition to these explicit costs or risks, managers using financial engineering should be mindful of other contingencies that are harder to quantify. As in other corporate transactions, there is some degree of credit risk because financially engineered solutions generally involve fallible counterparties. Financial engineers have devised various ways to mitigate credit risk, from collateralization agreements to AAA-rated derivative subsidiaries. Nevertheless, when you buy a commodity contract from a financial institution, you often are trading price risk for counterparty risk. A closely related problem arises from performance risk, or the risk that the counterparty in a commodity market will not be able to produce or deliver the product as specified in the contract.

Clearly, if TVA's proposed option contracts are to work as planned, its counter-parties must be able to deliver power.

Another contingency is basis risk, which you encounter when you cannot find a market that trades precisely the kind of risk you want to shed, and you have to use a close substitute that behaves similarly. ECT, Apache, and Amoco wrote contracts tied to specific grades of gas or oil, delivered at particular locations; users of these types of contracts may have to contend with differences between their individual exposure and the benchmarks in the industry. Other contracts might entail liquidity risks. For example, if a company uses short-term contracts to hedge long-term risks, the consequence may be sudden and unexpected cash-flow requirements. If so, a strategy intended to protect company value may turn out to be worse than no strategy at all. Perhaps the most troublesome risks that parties bear arise from legal, tax, and regulatory uncertainties. Courts, commissions, legislatures, and politicians may suddenly change the rules or simply abrogate existing contracts. As a result, it is not uncommon for "legal engineers" to work alongside financial engineers to ensure the reliability of their agreements.

## Making the Decision on Risk and Return

When a business decision is about to be made, it is always useful to repeat the mantra "risk and return." The two concepts are simple, but the cases presented here emphasize that a full understanding of how they are related often requires the collaboration of financial engineers and general strategists. Financial engineers can help to measure and moderate risks by answering such questions as, Based on the current market, what's a fair price for shedding oil-price risk? How much upside must I surrender to buy downside protection on a stock price? But ultimately, the most significant returns on transactions can be understood and valued only by the general manager, who must answer such questions as, What is it worth for the company to have its employees own stock? Will divesting a large part of our business allow us to make significant gains elsewhere? Each party has some of the relevant risk-and-return information. Working alone, neither the financial engineer nor the general manager has enough information to make a prudent decision. Working together, they may. What is most interesting about these five cases is not their technical virtuosity; to the contrary, the financial engineering employed was quite simple. Rather, the cases are exciting because they demonstrate that collaboration between financial engineers and general strategists can produce concepts and insights capable of meeting complex challenges.

The potential for this kind of collaboration will vary from company to company and from situation to situation. But the cases presented here should suggest that the possibilities are broader *The financial engineering* than might at first be imag- *used in these cases* ined. Equity derivatives that *was simple, but it solved* address employees' con- *complex problems.* cerns or signal confidence in a company's stock can be applied widely, as long as the company has traded common stock. The use of derivatives in an acquisition can be beneficial if the contract is structured around the subsequent accounting or stock market performance of the unit being sold. The use of futures markets and indices in commodity settings can also be applied much more broadly—for example, there are new real estate indices, as well as new derivative contracts on the indices. By using these contracts, a real estate brokerage could differentiate its services from those of its rivals by protecting a home seller or buyer against marketwide moves in prices between the time of listing and the time of sale or purchase.

Surely not all experiments in financial engineering will be successful. Some returns may be smaller than anticipated, some risks larger than expected. New technologies like computing or financial engineering usually produce winners and losers. In the case of computing, we remember the survivors—companies made richer by capitalizing on low-cost technology. Yet if we think back a decade or two, we also will remember companies whose experiments failed. Similarly, there are companies whose experiments with financial technology have been uninspiring. The debacles reported in the headlines represent our generation's technological washouts. What they seem to have in common is a degree of myopia on the part of senior management. We often learn that the specifications, design, execution, and oversight of these programs were all performed by the same technicians, without strategic direction and review. Facing a new specialty, senior managers sometimes throw their hands up and abdicate responsibility. The results are not surprising: An advanced financial program designed without reference to the business and its strategy, like a computer system built without input from end users, runs the risk of missing the mark.

The companies studied here adopted financial solutions as integral parts of their core business processes. The financial engineering used in these cases was remarkably simple, but it was able to solve complex managerial problems. Furthermore, these experiments with financial wizardry promise to accomplish the objectives that management established: capturing market share and profit with minimal risk, developing new production capacity, persuading employees and shareholders to buy stock, and bringing an important acquisition to completion. Although such success stories produce blander headlines than do dramatic tales of derivatives disasters, they should be more suggestive and inspiring to forward-thinking leaders

---

# What Is Financial Engineering?

ENGINEERING IS THE PRACTICAL application of mathematical or scientific principles to solve problems or design useful products and services. Engineers of all sorts get similar formal training in mathematics, then move on to their respective specializations. Civil engineers use their understanding of materials science and mechanics to design bridges; chemical engineers use their knowledge of chemical properties and interactions to design new compounds or make chemical processing plants more efficient. The financial engineer's knowledge base is financial economics, or the application of economic principles to the dynamics of securities markets, especially for the purpose of structuring, pricing, and managing the risk of financial contracts.

When designing a bridge, the civil engineer works within physical and budgetary constraints: Will the bridge support 50 trucks at once? Will it withstand extreme lateral forces of wind? Will it survive a once-a-century earthquake? How much will it cost? In designing a security or a risk-management strategy, the financial engineer also works within physical and budgetary constraints: Will this structure deliver the desired result even if the market moves suddenly and severely? How will it withstand a financial earthquake, such as a counterparty's default? How will it perform under current and future tax and accounting rules? How much will it cost? To succeed, both types of engineers must find optimal solutions within many different and often conflicting constraints.

These varied constraints lead to different solutions. Just as civil engineers can design various kinds of bridges, so financial engineers can design different kinds of financial instruments or strategies to produce a payoff. Robert C. Merton has presented a concrete example of the financial engineer's ability to design alternative routes to the same end, all fundamentally similar yet each with its own advantages and disadvantages (*Journal of Banking and Finance*, Volume 19, June 1995). Suppose that a professional investor wants to take a leveraged position in the Standard & Poor's 500 basket of U.S. stocks; Merton enumerates 11 ways of achieving that goal. Three are traditional do-it-yourself solutions in which the investor borrows to buy stock: buying each stock individually on the margin, borrowing to purchase shares in a Standard & Poor's 500 index mutual fund, or borrowing to buy a basket of stocks such as the American Stock Exchange's SPDR product. Three are products in which traditional financial intermediaries act as principals and offer payoffs that closely mimic the leveraged stock position; the actual products are structured as bank certificates of deposit, indexed notes, or variable-rate annuities. In five more alternatives, investors buy futures, forwards, swaps, or one of two different options on the Standard & Poor's 500 index, all of which are derivative contracts in that their payoffs are a function of (or are derived from) the value of an underlying index. Each of the 11 products or trading strategies can give the investor exposure to the stock market, and each produces functionally similar payoffs. The multitude of solutions exist because of the differing constraints facing the financial engineer.

Whereas derivatives have been traded for centuries, stretching back to the option contracts traded in Amsterdam in the seventeenth century, the modern field of financial engineering leaped forward in 1973, when Fisher Black, Myron Scholes, and Merton developed an approach to creating and valuing option contracts. In the same year, the Chicago Board of Exchange began the first modern market for options by trading calls on a dozen companies' shares. Following these pioneering steps in theory and practice, the past two decades have witnessed an explosion in research and in the understanding of how to structure, price, and manage the risks of derivative instruments.

Bridges occasionally collapse, sometimes because of poor engineering and other times because of bad luck. Except in extreme cases, it is often hard to distinguish between the two. Suppose that a bridge designed to withstand an earthquake of a certain size crumples after suffering a slightly larger shock. Is this calamity the result of poor engineering because the specifications should have been tighter, or of bad luck because an extremely improbable event occurred?

Financially engineered products also sometimes fail, and examining their wreckage to determine culpability is equally difficult. Some would contend that in 1987, portfolio insurance—a trading strategy designed to provide institutional investors with downside protection—

failed because it provided less than absolute protection. Yet if one looked closely at the "specifications" of the product as written by financial engineers before October 1987, it was clear that the strategy was not designed to cover all scenarios. In the aftermath of the crash, financial engineers have searched for alternative ways to deliver insurance. More recently, the failure of Metallgesellschaft's financially engineered hedging strategy has prompted much finger-pointing, litigation, and vigorous debate among practitioners and academics alike. The debate may never be resolved, but one can safely wager that clever financial engineers are working on ways to create alternative hedging strategies to avoid the problems that this incident exposed.

**Originally published in January–February 1996**
**Reprint 96112**

*The author would like to thank Timothy A. Luehrman and Donald S. Collat for their contributions to the field research cited in this article. He also gratefully acknowledges the support of the Global Financial Systems project at the Harvard Business School.*

# Transforming Corner-Office Strategy into Frontline Action

ORIT GADIESH AND JAMES L. GILBERT

## Executive Summary

WHEN CEOS PUSH DECISION MAKING out to the far reaches of an organization, good things happen: fleeting business opportunities are seized quickly and workers are motivated to innovate and take risks. But it's tricky to achieve both decentralized decision making and coherent strategic action at a company. If everyone is a decision maker, things can spin out of control.

In this article, Bain consultants Orit Gadiesh and James Gilbert explore the concept of the *strategic principle*—a memorable and actionable phrase that distills a company's corporate strategy into its unique essence and communicates it across an organization. If it's devised and disseminated properly, a strategic principle and empower employees to seize business opportunities but also focus everyone in an organization—executives and line manager alike—on the same strategic objectives.

153

The authors outline the three defining characteristics of a good strategic principle—it should force trade-offs between competing resource demands, it should serve as a test for the strategic soundness of a particular action, and it should set clear boundaries for employees to operate within even as it grants them freedom to experiment. They explain how mangers can create a strategic principle, how they should test it, and when they should revisit it.

The authors present real-world examples of how companies use their strategic principles. For instance, they describe how Southwest Airlines stopped flying to Denver after it measured the high costs of providing flight service in that part of the country against its strategic principle of offering customers short-haul air travel at fares competitive with the cost of automobile travel.

This tool is increasingly useful in today's rapidly changing business environment, the authors conclude, and it is likely to become even more crucial to corporate success.

---

*It's a challenge that confronts every company, large and small: how do you give employees clear strategic direction but also inspire flexibility and risk taking? One answer is to create and broadcast a "strategic principle"—a pithy, memorable distillation of strategy that guides employees as it empowers them.*

WE ALL KNOW THE BENEFITS OF pushing decision making from the CEO's office out to the far reaches of an organization. Fleeting business opportunities can be seized quickly. Products and services better reflect subtle shifts in customers' preferences. Empowered workers are motivated to innovate and take risks.

But while the value of such an approach is clear, particularly in a volatile business environment, there is also a built-in risk: an organization in which everyone is a decision maker has the potential to spin out of control. Within a single company, it's tricky to achieve both decentralized decision making and coherent strategic action. Still, some companies—think General Electric, America Online, Vanguard, Dell, Wal-Mart, Southwest Airlines, and eBay—have done just that.

These companies employ what we call a *strategic principle*, a memorable and actionable phrase that distills a company's corporate strategy into its unique essence and communicates it throughout the organization. (For a list of companies' strategic principles, see the exhibit "It's All in a Phrase.")

---

### It's All in a Phrase

*A handful of companies have distilled their strategy into a phrase and have used it to drive consistent strategic action throughout their organizations.*

| Company | Strategic Principle |
|---|---|
| America Online | Consumer connectivity first—anytime, anywhere |
| Dell | Be direct |
| eBay | Focus on trading communities |
| General Electric | Be number one or number two in every industry in which we compete, or get out |
| Southwest Airlines | Meet customers' short-haul travel needs at fares competitive with the cost of automobile travel |
| Vanguard | Unmatchable value for the investor-owner |
| Wal-Mart | Low prices, every day |

This tool—which we have observed in use at about a dozen companies, even though they don't label it as such—would always serve a company well. But it has become particularly useful in today's rapidly and constantly changing business environment. Indeed, in our conversations and work with more than 50 CEOs over the past two years, we have come to appreciate the strategic principle's power—its ability to help companies maintain strategic focus while fostering the flexibility among employees that permits innovation and a rapid response to opportunities. Strategic principles are likely to become even more crucial to corporate success in the years ahead.

## Distillation and Communication

To better understand what a strategic principle is and how it can be used, it may be helpful to look at a military analogy: the rules of engagement for battle. For example, Admiral Lord Nelson's crews in Britain's eighteenth-century wars against the French were guided by a simple strategic principle: whatever you do, get alongside an enemy ship.

The Royal Navy's seamanship, training, and experience gave it the advantage every time it engaged one-on-one against any of Europe's lesser fleets. So Nelson rejected as impractical the common practice of an admiral attempting to control a fleet through the use of flag signals. Instead, he gave his captains strategic parameters—they knew they had to battle rival ships one-on-one—leaving them to determine exactly how to engage in such combat. By using a strategic principle instead of explicit signals to direct his forces, Nelson consistently defeated the French, including a great victory in the dark of night, when signals would have been useless. Nelson's rule of engagement was simple enough for every one of his officers and sailors to know by heart. And it was enduring, a valid directive that was good until the relative naval capabilities of Britain and its rivals changed.

The distillation of a company's strategy into a pithy, memorable, and prescriptive phrase is important because a brilliant business strategy, like an insightful approach to warfare, is of little use unless people understand it well enough to apply it—both to anticipated decisions and unforeseen opportunities. In our work, we often see evidence of what we call the 80-100 rule: you're better off with a strategy that is 80% right and 100% implemented than one that is 100% right but doesn't drive consistent action throughout the company. A strategic principle can help a company balance that ratio.

The beauty of having a corporate strategic principle— a company should have only one—is that everyone in an organization, the executives in the front office as well as people in the operating units, can knowingly work toward the same strategic objective without being rigid about how they do so. Decisions don't always have to make the slow trip to and from the executive suite. When a strategic principle is well crafted and effectively communicated, managers at all levels can be trusted to make decisions that advance rather than undermine company strategy.

Given what we've said so far, a strategic principle might seem to be a mission statement by another name. But while both help employees understand a company's direction, the two are different tools that communicate different things. A mission statement informs a company's *culture*. A strategic principle drives a company's *strategy*. A mission statement is *aspirational*: it gives people something to strive for. A strategic principle is *action oriented*: it enables people to do something now. A mission statement is meant to *inspire* frontline workers. A strategic principle enables them to *act* quickly by giving them explicit guidance to make strategically consistent choices.

Consider the difference between GE's mission statement and its strategic principle. The company's mission statement exhorts GE's leaders—"always with unyielding integrity"—to be "passionately focused on driving customer success" and to "create an environment of 'stretch,' excitement, informality, and trust," among other things. The language is aspirational and emotional. By contrast, GE's well-known strategic principle—"Be number one or number two in every industry in which we compete, or get out"—is action oriented. The first part of the phrase is an explicit strategic challenge, and the second part leaves no question in line managers' minds about what they should do.

## Three Defining Attributes

A strategic principle, as the distillation of a company's strategy, should guide a company's allocation of scarce resources—capital, time, management's attention, labor, and brand—in order to build a sustainable competitive advantage. It should tell a company what to do and, just as important, what not to do. More specifically, an effective strategic principle does the following:

- It forces trade-offs between competing resource demands;

- It tests the strategic soundness of a particular action;

- It sets clear boundaries within which employees must operate while granting them freedom to experiment within those constraints.

These three qualities can be seen in America Online's strategic principle. CEO Steve Case says personal interaction on-line is the soul of the Internet, and he has positioned AOL to create that interaction. Thus, AOL's strategic principle in the years leading up to its recent merger with Time Warner has been "Consumer connectivity first—anytime, anywhere."

This strategic principle has helped AOL make tough choices when allocating its resources. For example, in 1997, the company needed cash to grow, so it sold off its network infrastructure and outsourced that capability— a risky move at a time when it appeared that network ownership might be the key to success on the Internet. In keeping with its strategic principle, AOL instead spent its time and cash on improving connectivity at its Web site, focusing particularly on access, navigation, and interaction. As a result, it avoided investing capital in what turned out to be a relatively low-return business.

Its strategic principle has also helped AOL test whether a given business move makes strategic sense. For instance, the Internet company has chosen to expand its global network through alliances with local partners, even though that approach can take longer than simply transplanting AOL's own technology and know-how. AOL acknowledges that a local partner better understands the native culture and community, which is essential for connecting with customers.

Finally, AOL's strategic principle has spurred focused experimentation in the field by clearly defining employees' latitude for making moves. For example, AOL's former vice president of marketing, Jan Brandt, mailed more than 250 million AOL diskettes to consumers nationwide. The innovative campaign turned the company into one of the best-known names in cyberspace—all because Brandt, now AOL's vice chair and chief marketing officer, guided by the principle of connecting consumers, put her resources into empowering AOL's target community rather than sinking time and money into slick advertising.

As AOL's experience illustrates, a strong strategic principle can inform high-level corporate decisions—those involving divestitures, for example—as well as decisions made by department heads or others further down in an organization. It also frees up CEOs from constant involvement in the implementation of their strategic mandates. "The genius of a great leader is to leave behind him a situation that common sense, without the grace of genius, can deal with successfully," said journalist and political thinker Walter Lippman. Scratch the surface of a number of high-performing companies, and you'll find that strategic principles are connecting the strategic insights—if not always the genius—of leaders with the pragmatic sense of line operators.

## Now More Than Ever

In the past, a strategic principle was nice to have but was hardly required, unless a company found itself in a trying business situation. Today, many companies simultaneously face four situations that make a strategic principle crucial for success: decentralization, rapid growth, technological change, and institutional turmoil.

For the reasons mentioned above, *decentralization* is becoming common at companies of all stripes; thus, there is a corresponding need for a mechanism to ensure coherent strategic action. Especially in the case of diversified conglomerates, where strategy is formed in each of the business units, a strategic principle can help executives maintain consistency while giving unit managers the freedom to tailor their strategies to meet their own needs. It can also clarify the value of the center at such far-flung companies. For example, GE's long-standing strategic principle of always being number one or number two in an industry offers a powerful rationale for how a conglomerate can create value but still give individual units considerable strategic freedom.

A strategic principle is also crucial when a company is experiencing *rapid growth*. During such times, it's increasingly the case that less-experienced managers are forced to make decisions about nettlesome issues for which there may be no precedent. A clear and precise strategic principle can help counteract this shortage of experience. This is particularly true when a start-up company is growing rapidly in an established industry. For instance, as Southwest Airlines began to grow quickly, it might have been tempted to mimic its rivals' ultimately unsuccessful strategies if it hadn't had its own strategic principle to follow: "Meet customers' short-haul travel needs at fares competitive with the cost of automobile travel." Likewise, eBay, whose principle is "Focus on trading communities," might have been tempted, like many Internet marketplaces, to diversify into all sorts of services. But eBay has chosen to outsource certain services—for instance, management of the photos that sellers post on the site to illustrate the items they put up for bid—while it continues to invest in services like Bill-point, which lets sellers accept credit-card payments from bidders. EBay's strategic principle has ensured that the entire company stays focused on the core trading business.

The staggering pace of *technological change* over the past decade has been costly for companies that don't have a strategic principle. Never before in business has there been more uncertainty combined with so great an emphasis on speed. Managers in high-tech industries in particular must react immediately to sudden and unexpected developments. Often, the sum of the reactions across the organization ends up defining the company's strategic course. A strategic principle—for example, Dell's mandate to sell direct to end users—helps ensure that the decisions made by frontline managers in such circumstances add up to a consistent, coherent strategy.

Finally, a strategic principle can help provide continuity during periods of *organizational turmoil.* An increasingly common example of turmoil in this era of short-term CEOs is leadership succession. A new CEO can bring with him or her a new strategy—but not necessarily a new strategic principle. For instance, when Jack Brennan took over as chairman and CEO at Vanguard five years ago, the strategic transition was seamless, despite some tension around the leadership transition. He maintained the mutual fund company's strategic principle—"Unmatchable value for the investor-owner"—thereby allowing managers to pursue their strategic objectives without many of the distractions so often associated with leadership changes. (For our own experience with organizational turmoil and strategic principles, see "Bain & Company: Case Study of a Strategic Principle" at the end of this article.)

# Strategic Principles in Action

Strategic principles and their benefits can best be understood by seeing the results they create.

## FORCING TRADE-OFFS AT SOUTHWEST AIRLINES

Southwest Airlines is one of the air-travel industry's great success stories. It is the only airline that hasn't lost money in the past 25 years. Its stock price rose a compounded 21,000% between 1972 and 1992, and it is up 300% over the past five years, which have been difficult ones in the airline industry. For most companies, such rapid growth would cause problems: legions of frontline employees taking up the mantle of decision making from core executives and, inevitably, stumbling. But in Southwest's case, employees have consistently made trade-offs in keeping with the company's strategic principle.

The process for making important and complicated decisions about things like network design, service offerings, route selection and pricing, cabin design, and ticketing procedures is straightforward. That's because the trade-offs required by the strategic principle are clear. For instance, in 1983, Southwest initiated service to Denver, a potentially high-traffic destination and a seemingly sensible expansion of the company's presence in the Southwestern United States. However, the airline experienced longer and more consistent delays at Denver's Stapleton airport than it did anywhere else. These delays were caused not by slow turnaround at the gate but by increased taxi time on the runway and planes circling in the air because of bad weather. Southwest had to decide whether the potential growth from serving the Denver market was worth the higher costs associated with the delays, which would ultimately be reflected in higher ticket prices. The company turned to its strategic principle: would the airline be able to maintain fares competitive with the cost of automobile travel? Clearly, in Denver at least, it couldn't. Southwest pulled out of Stapleton three years after inaugurating the service there and has not returned.

## TESTING ACTION AT AOL

A large part of AOL's ability to move so far and so fast across untrod ground lies in its practice of testing potential moves against its strategic principle. Employees who see attractive opportunities can ask themselves whether seizing one or several will lead to deeper consumer connectivity or broader distribution. Take, for example, line manager Katherine Borescnik, now president of programming at AOL. Several years ago she noticed increased activity—call it consumer connectivity—around the bulletin-board folders created on the site by two irreverent stock analysts and AOL subscribers. She offered the analysts the chance to create their own financial site, which became Motley Fool, a point of connection and information for do-it-yourself investors.

And AOL's strategic principle reaches even deeper into the organization. The hundreds of acquisitions and deals that AOL has made in the past few years have involved numerous employees. While top officers make final decisions, employees on the ground first screen opportunities against the company's strategic principle. Furthermore, the integration efforts following acquisitions, while choreographed at the top, are executed by a coterie of managers who ensure that the plans comply with the company's strategic principle. "We have succeeded, both in our deal making and in our integration, because our acquisitions have all been driven by our focus on how our customers communicate and connect," says Ken Novack, AOL Time Warner's vice chairman.

AOL's massive merger with Time Warner clearly furthers AOL's strategic principle of enabling consumer connections "anytime, anywhere" by adding TV and cable access to the Internet company's current dial-up access on the personal computer. But integrating this merger, which will involve hundreds of employees making and executing thousands of decisions, may be the ultimate test of AOL's strategic principle.

## EXPERIMENTING WITHIN BOUNDARIES AT VANGUARD

The Vanguard Group, with $565 billion in assets under management, has quietly become a giant in the mutual fund industry. The company's strategy is a response to the inability of most mutual funds to beat the market, often because of the cost of their marketing activities, overhead, and frequent transactions. To counter this, Vanguard discourages investors from making frequent trades and keeps its own overhead and advertising costs far below the industry average. It passes the savings directly to investors, who, because Vanguard is a mutual rather than a public company, are the fund's owners.

While this was Vanguard's founding strategy, for years the company didn't communicate it widely to employees. As a result, they often suggested initiatives that were out of sync with the company's core strategy. "Midlevel managers would walk in holding the newspaper saying, 'Look at what Fidelity just did. How about if we do that?'" Jack Brennan says. It wasn't apparent to them that Vanguard's strategy was very different from that of its rival, which has higher costs and isn't mutually owned. Over the years, Vanguard has invested considerable energy in crafting a strategic principle and using it to disseminate the company's strategy. Now, because employees understand the strategy, top management trusts them to initiate moves on their own.

Consider Vanguard's response to a major trend in retail fund distribution: the emergence of the on-line channel. Industry surveys indicated that most investors wanted Internet access to their accounts and that on-line traders were more active than off-line traders. So Vanguard chose to integrate the Internet into its service in a way that furthered its strategy of keeping costs low: basically, it lets customers access their accounts on-line, but it limits Web-based trading. It should be noted that the original ideas for Vanguard's on-line initiatives, including early ventures with AOL, were conceived by frontline employees, not senior executives.

Brennan says the company's strategic principle affects the entire management process, including hiring, training, performance measurement, and incentives. He points to a hidden benefit of having a strong strategic principle: "You're more efficient and can run with a leaner management team because everyone is on the same page."

## Creating a Strategic Principle

Many of the best and most conspicuous examples of strategic principles come from companies that were founded on them, companies such as eBay, Dell, Vanguard, Southwest Airlines, and Wal-Mart ("Low prices, every day"). The founders of those companies espoused a clear guiding principle that summarized the essence of what would become a full-blown business strategy. They attracted investors who believed it, hired employees who bought into it, and targeted customers who wanted it.

Leaders of long-standing multinationals, like GE, crafted their strategic principles at a critical juncture: when increasing corporate complexity threatened to confuse priorities on the front line and obscure the essence that truly differentiated their strategy from that of their rivals.

Companies in this second category, which represents most of the companies that are likely to contemplate creating a strategic principle, face a demanding exercise. It probably comes as no surprise that identifying the essence of your strategy so it can be translated into a simple, memorable phrase is no easy task. It's a bit like corporate genomics: the principle must isolate and capture the corporate equivalent of the genetic code that differentiates your company from its competitors. This is somewhat like identifying the 2% of DNA that separates man from monkey—or, even more difficult and more apt, the .1% of DNA that differentiates each human being.

There are different ways to identify the elements that must be captured in a strategic principle, but keep in mind that a corporate strategy represents a plan to effectively allocate scarce resources to achieve sustainable competitive advantage. Managers need to ask themselves: how does my company allocate those resources to create value in a unique way, one that differentiates my company from competitors? Try to summarize the answer in a brief phrase that captures the essence of your company's point of differentiation.

Once that idea has been expressed in a phrase, test the strategic principle for its enduring nature. Does it capture what you intend to do for only the next three to five years, or does it capture a more timeless essence: the genetic code of your company's competitive differentiation? Then test the strategic principle for its communicative power. Is it clear, concise, and memorable? Would you feel proud to paint it on the side of a truck, as Wal-Mart does?

Finally, test the principle for its ability to promote and guide action. In particular, assess whether it exhibits the three attributes of an effective strategic principle. Will it force trade-offs? Will it serve as a test for the wisdom of a particular business move, especially one that might promote short-term profits at the expense of long-term strategy? Does it set boundaries within which people will nonetheless be free to experiment?

Given the importance of getting your strategic principle right, it is wise to gather feedback on these questions from executives and other employees during an incubation period. Once you are satisfied that the statement is accurate and compelling, disseminate it throughout the organization.

Of course, just as a brilliant strategy is worthless unless it is implemented, a powerful strategic principle is of no use unless it is communicated effectively. When CEO Jack Welch talks about aligning employees around GE's strategy and values, he emphasizes the need for consistency, simplicity, and repetition. The approach is neither flashy nor complicated, but it takes enormous discipline and could scarcely be more important. Welch has so broadly evangelized GE's "Be number one or number two" strategic principle that employees are not the only ones to chant the rant. So can most business writers, MBA students, and managers at other companies.

## When Rethinking Is Required

No strategy is eternal, nor is any strategic principle. But even if the elements of your strategy change, the very essence of it is likely to remain the same. Thus, your strategy may shift substantially as your customers' demographics and needs change. It may have to be modified in light of your company's changing costs and assets compared with those of competitors. Strategic half-lives are shortening, and, in general, strategy should be reviewed every quarter and updated every year. But while it's worth revisiting your strategic principle every time you reexamine your strategy, it is likely to change only when there is a significant shift in the basic economics and opportunities of your market caused by, say, legislation or a completely new technology or business model.

Even then, your strategic principle may need only refining or expanding. GE's strategic principle has been enhanced, but not replaced, since Welch articulated it in 1981. Similarly, AOL's strategic principle will need to be broadened, but not necessarily jettisoned, following its merger with Time Warner. Ultimately, the merged company's strategic principle will also need to embody the importance of high-quality and relevant content, Time Warner's hallmark.

Vanguard takes explicit steps to ensure that the direction provided by its strategic principle remains current. For example, as part of an internal "devil's advocacy" process, managers are divided into groups to critique and defend past decisions and current policies. Recently, the group reconsidered two major strategic policies: the prohibitions against opening branch offices and against acquiring money management firms. After considerable discussion, the policies remained in place. According to CEO Brennan, "Sometimes the greatest value [of revisiting our strategic principle] is reconfirming what we're already doing." At the same time, Vanguard has the process to identify when change is needed.

## Fundamental Principles

Respondents to Bain's annual survey of executives on the usefulness of management tools repeatedly cite the key role a mission statement can play in a company's success. We agree that a mission statement is crucial for promulgating a company's values and building a robust corporate culture. But it still leaves a large gap in a company's management communications portfolio. At least as important as a mission statement is something that promulgates a company's strategy—that is, a strategic principle.

The ability of frontline employees to execute a company's strategy without close central oversight is vital as the pace of technological change accelerates and as companies grow rapidly and become increasingly decentralized. To drive such behavior, a company needs to give employees a mandate broad enough to encourage enterprising behavior but specific enough to align employees' initiatives with company strategy.

While not a perfect analogy, the U.S. Constitution is in some ways like a strategic principle. It articulates and embodies the essence of the country's "strategy"— to guarantee liberty and justice for all of its citizens— while providing direction to those drafting the laws and regulations that implement the strategy. While no corporate strategy has liberty and justice at its heart, the elements of an effective strategy are just as central to the success of a company as those concepts are to the prosperity of the United States. And in neither case will success be realized unless the core strategy is communicated broadly and effectively.

---

## Bain & Company: Case Study of a Strategic Principle

I LEARNED THE MOST ABOUT strategic principles in the trenches at Bain & Company when, a decade ago, we almost went bankrupt.

Bill Bain founded Bain & Company nearly 30 years ago on the basis of a simple but powerful notion: "The product of a consultant should be results for clients—not reports." Over time, this mandate to deliver results through strategy became Bain's strategic principle. It remains so today.

This directive fosters specific action, as an effective strategic principle should. It means that, from the very beginning of an assignment, you are constantly thinking about how a recommendation will get implemented. It also requires you to tell clients the truth, even if it's difficult, because you can't achieve results by whitewashing problems. And this strategic principle has teeth: Bain has always measured partners' performance according to the results they achieve for their clients, not just on billings to the firm.

That was the company I joined. And for many years it grew rapidly, all the time guided by its strategic principle. Then, just over a decade ago, the founding partners decided to get their money out and sold 30% of the firm to an employee stock-option plan. This saddled us with hundreds of millions of dollars of debt and tens of millions of dollars of interest payments. The move, whose details initially were not disclosed to the rest of us, was based on the assumption that the company would continue its historic growth rate of 50% a year, which couldn't be sustained at the size we had become. When growth slowed, the details came to light.

The nonfounding partners faced a critical choice. Everybody had attractive offers. Competitors and the press predicted we wouldn't survive. Recruits and clients were watchful. To make a long story short, we sat down around a conference table and resolved to turn the company around. The key to doing that, we decided, was to stick with our strategic principle.

What followed was a couple of years during which adhering to that goal was achingly difficult. But doing so forced important trade-offs. In one case, right in the middle of the crisis, we pulled out of a major assignment that was inconsistent with our principle. We believed the projects that the client was determined to undertake could not produce significant results for the company. Today, we all believe that had we veered from our principle in that instance, we would not be around.

More recently, our strategic principle has freed us to explore other ventures. Seven years ago, for instance, we became interested in private equity consulting, quite a different business from serving corporate clients. We initially struggled with the notion but quickly realized that it fit our strategic principle of delivering results through strategy, only to a new client segment. We knew that we could trust our colleagues forming the practice area to act consistently with the company's broader goals because the strategic principle was fundamental to their perspective. The strength of our shared principle permitted us to experiment and ultimately develop a successful new practice area.

Our principle continues to let partners develop new practices, markets, and interests quickly and without splintering the firm. It has given us the capacity to evolve and endure.

**Orit Gadiesh**

**Originally published in May 2001**
**Reprint R0105**

*Bain consultant Coleman Mark assisted with this article.*

# Where Value Lives in a Networked World

MOHANBIR SAWHNEY AND DEVAL PARIKH

## Executive Summary

WHILE MANY MANAGEMENT THINKERS proclaim an era of radical uncertainty, authors Sawhney and Parikh assert that the seemingly endless upheavals of the digital age are more predictable than that: today's changes have a common root, and that root lies in the nature of intelligence in networks. Understanding the patterns of intelligence migration can help companies decipher and plan for the inevitable disruptions in today's business environment.

Two patterns in network intelligence are reshaping industries and organizations. First, intelligence is decoupling—that is, modern high-speed networks are pushing back-end intelligence and front-end intelligence toward opposite ends of the network, making the ends the two major sources of potential profits. Second, intelligence is becoming more fluid and modular. Small units of intelligence now float freely like molecules in the ether, coalescing into temporary bundles whenever and wherever necessary to solve problems.

The authors present four strategies that companies can use to profit from these patterns: *arbitrage* allows companies to move intelligence to new regions or countries where the cost of maintaining intelligence is lower; *aggregation* combines formerly isolated pieces of infrastructure intelligence into a large pool of shared infrastructure provided over a network; *rewiring* allows companies to connect islands of intelligence by creating common information backbones; and *reassembly* allows businesses to reorganize pieces of intelligence into coherent, personalized packages for customers.

By being aware of patterns in network intelligence and by acting rather than reacting, companies can turn chaos into opportunity, say the authors.

---

IN RECENT YEARS, IT SEEMS as though the only constant in business has been upheaval. Changes have occurred at every level, from the way entire industries are structured, to the way companies interact with customers, to the way basic tasks are carried out in individual organizations. In response, many managers and management thinkers have thrown up their hands, proclaiming an era of radical uncertainty. Business has become so complex, they say, that trying to predict what lies ahead is futile. Plotting strategy is a fool's game. The best you can do is

*Network intelligence is the Rosetta Stone that can enable executives and entrepreneurs to decipher many of the phenomena shaping the future of business.*

become as flexible as possible and hope you'll be able to ride out the waves of disruption.

There's some truth in that view. The business world has become much more complicated, and the ability to adapt and respond is now as important as the ability to anticipate and act. But we take issue with the assumption that the changes we've been seeing are random, disconnected events and thus unpredictable. We have studied the myriad upheavals taking place in business, and we've concluded that many of them have a common root, which lies in the nature of intelligence in networks. Put simply, the digitization of information, combined with advances in computing and communications, has fundamentally changed how all networks operate, human as well as technological, and that change is having profound consequences for the way work is done and value is created throughout the economy. Network intelligence is the Rosetta Stone that can enable executives and entrepreneurs to decipher many of the phenomena shaping the future of business.

The evolution in network intelligence may sound like an awfully abstract topic, but it has immediate and very concrete implications. The future of many technology companies, from Dell to AT&T to hordes of Internet start-ups, hinges on their ability to recognize and adapt to shifts in network intelligence. And even if your company is not directly involved in the communications or computing business, it will not be immune to the impact of shifts in network intelligence. In a highly connected world, the location and mobility of network intelligence directly influences the way companies organize their people, market products, manage information, and work with partners. "The network is the computer," Sun Microsystems has famously proclaimed. We would go even further: the network is the economy.

# Intelligence in the Network

Let's start with some basic definitions. A network is a conduit for information; it can be as simple as two tin cans tied together with a string or as complicated as the Internet. The intelligence of a network is its functionality—its ability to distribute, store, assemble, or modify information. A simple analog network, like the two tin cans, is considered "dumb"; it's just a pipe that transports information without enhancing it. A complex digital network, like the Internet, is "smart"; it can improve the utility of information in multiple ways. That's crucially important for one simple reason: in an information economy, improving the utility of information is synonymous with creating economic value. Where intelligence resides, so too does value.

As networking technologies have advanced in recent years, both the location and the mobility of network intelligence have changed dramatically. (See the exhibit "The Two Patterns in Intelligence Migration.") By understanding the patterns underlying those changes, you can gain valuable insight into the way economic value is shifting across industries and among companies. And that knowledge can help you to act while others merely react.

## THE DECOUPLING OF INTELLIGENCE

In the absence of a network, intelligence is static; it can be applied only where it lives. If different kinds of intelligence are needed to perform a task, they must all be bundled together in the same place. For instance, a personal computer not connected to a network has to contain all the intelligence needed to process, store, and display information for a wide variety of user tasks. But the nature of the front-end intelligence needed to interact with users is very different from the nature of the back-end intelligence needed to process and store information. The user wants a computer that is easy to use, portable, flexible, and personalizable. But under the hood, the machine needs to be powerful, reliable, and easy to maintain. The bundling of these two types of

---

## The Two Patterns in Intelligence Migration

As network technologies have advanced in recent years, both the location and the mobility of network intelligence have changed dramatically. As for location, back-end intelligence becomes embedded in a shared infrastructure at the network's core, while front-end intelligence fragments into many different forms at the network's periphery, where the users are. As for mobility, large units of intelligence that were once disconnected become small units of freefloating intelligence that coalesce into temporary bundles whenever and wherever necessary to solve problems.

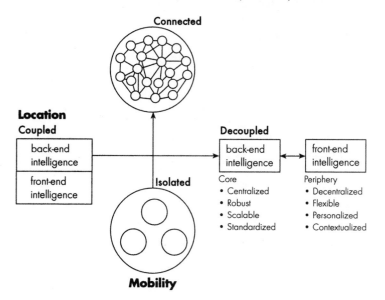

intelligence necessitates compromises in design. For a laptop computer to be light and portable, for instance, it cannot have the most powerful microprocessor, a motherboard capable of additional slots, or a very large hard disk for storage.

When a PC is networked, however, it is no longer necessary for the different types of intelligence to be combined. Front-end intelligence can be separated from back-end intelligence. Instead of being replicated on every individual PC, the back-end intelligence can be consolidated onto powerful, efficient, and reliable network servers. And the front-end intelligence, freed from basic processing functions, can be much more customized to particular people and tasks. The PC can morph from a single jack-of-all-trades-master-of-none machine into an array of small, specialized electronic tools.

In more general terms, modern high-speed networks push back-end intelligence and front-end intelligence in two different directions, toward opposite ends of the network. Back-end intelligence becomes embedded into a shared infrastructure at the core of the network, while front-end intelligence fragments into many different forms at the periphery of the network, where the users are. And since value follows intelligence, the two ends of the network become the major sources of potential profits. The middle of the network gets hollowed out; it becomes a dumb conduit, with little potential for value creation. Moreover, as value diverges, so do companies and competition. Organizations that once incorporated diverse units focused on both back-end

*In a networked world, more money can be made in managing interactions than in performing actions.*

processing and front-end customer management split into separate infrastructure and customer-relationship management businesses, with very different capabilities and strategies.[1] (See "Value Trends in the Network Age" at the end of this article.)

## THE MOBILIZATION OF INTELLIGENCE

In a connected world, intelligence becomes fluid and modular. Small units of intelligence float freely like molecules in the ether, coalescing into temporary bundles whenever and wherever necessary to solve problems. Consider SETI@home, a project launched by the University of California at Berkeley to search for extraterrestrial life. Radio signals received by the world's biggest telescope dish—the 1,000-foot Arecibo Observatory in Puerto Rico—are carved into 330-kilobyte "work units" and distributed over the Internet to PCs around the world. Individual computer owners donate their spare computing cycles—their processing intelligence—to the project by allowing their computers to analyze data in the background or when idle. Within a year of its launch in May 1999, more than 2 million people in 226 countries had provided about 280,000 years of computer time to the effort. SETI@home has a total computing power of roughly 12 teraflops, making it four times as powerful as the world's fastest supercomputer. The network makes it possible to pool the intelligence residing in millions of computers across the globe into an ad hoc system with massive computing capability.

The mobilization of intelligence has profound organizational implications. Connected by networks, different companies can easily combine their capabilities and

resources into temporary and flexible alliances to capitalize on particular market opportunities. As these "plug-
and-play" enterprises become common, value shifts from
entities that own intelligence to those that orchestrate
the flow and combination of intelligence. In other words,
more money can be made in managing interactions than
in performing actions. That explains why companies like
Cisco and Hewlett-Packard are evolving into intelligent
hubs that coordinate the interactions among a network
of channel partners, suppliers, and customers. By connecting the business processes of manufacturing service
providers like Solectron and Flextronics to the business
processes of channel partners and customers, Cisco and
HP are able to coordinate the intelligent flow of information in their business networks. As a consequence, they
are able to extract the bulk of the value created by the
network, much as the conductor of a symphony orches-
tra garners the lion's share of the audience's applause.

Just as the decoupling of intelligence requires a reliable high-speed network, the mobilization of intelligence
requires a common language. Without the existence of
universal protocols for information exchange, individual
pieces of intelligence cannot communicate and collaborate. For instance, the mobilization of intelligence
among devices requires device-to-device communication
protocols like Bluetooth and Jini. The mobilization of
intelligence from the Internet to wireless devices
requires protocols like the Wireless Applications Protocol (WAP). And the organization of plug-and-play business networks requires the widespread adoption of protocols for describing products and processes like
Extensible Markup Language (XML). The development
of these and other network standards will play a large
role in determining the future shape of business.

# Reshaping Industries

The decoupling and mobilization of intelligence are changing the competitive landscapes of many large industries. The most dramatic effects, not surprisingly, are being felt in network-based businesses like telecommunications. When traditional telephone companies built their analog systems, they had to bundle many different kinds of intelligence—for processing, transport, and user functionality—into the middle of their networks. The wires needed to be smart because the user device was dumb—a simple rotary phone. But the emergence of digital networks based on the Internet Protocol (IP) has turned the old networks into huge, expensive albatrosses around the phone companies' necks. Because intelligence can now be embedded in servers, software, and intelligent devices located at the core as well as at the periphery of the network, the middle of the network can and should be dumb. All that's needed is a fast and reliable pipe, with a little bit of routing intelligence.

This shift poses a grave threat to service providers like AT&T, which rely on voice and data transport for the bulk of their revenues. As transport becomes a commodity, rates for long-distance telephony are plummeting. Start-ups like Dialpad and Go2Call are even offering free PC-to-phone long-distance service over the Internet. The real value in telecommunications is shifting to the ends of the network. At the core, infrastructure providers like Sun, Cisco, Nortel, and Lucent are earning big profits. And at the periphery, companies like Yahoo!, InfoSpace, America Online, and Phone.com are extracting value by controlling the user interface and managing customer relationships. Even in the emerging broadband and wireless arenas, service

providers will find it difficult to make money just by
selling access to the Internet. They will have to provide
value-added infrastructure services—like hosting, systems integration, and network maintenance—or find a
way to earn commissions on the transactions that flow
through their pipes.

The computing business is going through a similar
transformation. The functionality that was once built
into computers or sold as software packages can now be
delivered over the Internet, much as utility companies
deliver electricity through power lines. Just as corporations and consumers no longer need to own their own
generators, they'll soon be freed from having to own their
own computing hardware and applications. Already,
consumers can use Yahoo!'s servers to store their e-mail
messages, calendars, address books, digital photographs,
digital wallets, faxes, and data files. And businesses can
now purchase, on an as-needed basis, the computer
applications required for customer service, human
resource management, accounting, and payroll from outside service providers.

Obviously, this trend has profound implications for
traditional hardware and software companies. To go
where the value is, they'll have to transform themselves
from product companies to service providers, or they'll
have to shift their focus from
selling primarily to end users
to selling to the big infrastructure providers like
Yahoo! and Exodus. Dell
Computer, in a major effort
to reinvent itself, is taking
both paths. In February 2000, Dell announced a series of
initiatives called "Dell E Works" aimed at broadening

*It may now make more
sense to talk about a
company's "distributed
capabilities" instead
of its "core capabilities."*

its revenue base beyond traditional hardware. It now offers its enterprise systems and storage products over the Internet through its Dell Hosting Service, and it is expanding into services like e-consulting and Web hosting. It is also enlarging its customer base to include Internet service providers (ISPs) and hosting companies that provide computing as a utility. As part of this effort, it is moving beyond its reliance on the Windows operating system by embracing Linux, an OS better suited to running the robust servers owned by the computing utilities. The new initiatives are already paying off. In the quarter that ended July 28, 2000, Dell's "beyond the box" revenues increased 40% from the previous year, accounting for 16% of the company's net revenues.

## Reshaping Companies

The impact of intelligence migration is being felt within companies as well as across industries. The shrinking of middle management in many organizations, for example, is another manifestation of the hollowing of the middle, as intelligence gets pushed to the core (in this case, top management) and the periphery (front-line employees). Before robust digital networks and easy-to-use collaboration tools like e-mail, groupware, and intranets existed, it was difficult to communicate information through a large organization. So a lot of middle managers were needed to package and distribute information between top management and frontline employees. But now that people are connected electronically, information and intelligence can be transported more seamlessly. As a result, the information-transport function of middle managers has become superfluous. Just as the telecom network can have dumb pipes with intelligent ends, the organization can have a dumb information network that allows senior managers to communicate directly with frontline employees. Leadership and strategy get centralized at the top management level, while the ability to act and make decisions is pushed to the periphery of the organization. The challenge for the remaining middle managers is to redefine their roles as coordinators, facilitators, organizers, and mentors—to provide new kinds of organizational intelligence.

The mobilization of intelligence is having other organizational effects as well. Rather than being centralized in discrete units, a company's capabilities are becoming more distributed and more modular. The Internet lets geographically dispersed individuals and teams connect to solve customer problems or respond quickly to market opportunities. A company can, for example, locate its R&D capabilities in Silicon Valley, its engineering capabilities in India, its manufacturing capabilities in China, and its customer-support capabilities in Ireland. The interaction of the far-flung units is mediated, moment by moment, by the network, not by a large, expensive, and slow-moving managerial staff. In fact, it may now make more sense to talk about a company's "distributed capabilities" instead of its "core capabilities." (See "Network Intelligence in the Public Sector" at the end of this article.)

The same kind of flexible collaboration is also changing business-to-business interactions. We see it in the sharing of Internet-based business infrastructures. Direct competitors are, for example, coming together to share supply chain platforms by forming consortia like Covisint (in the automobile industry), Envera (in the chemicals industry), and Transora (in the packaged-goods industry). We see it as well in the packaging of corporate capabilities, such as FedEx's order tracking functionality and General Electric's consumable supplies ordering, as modules that other companies can purchase and plug in to their own operations. More profoundly, the ability to creatively combine capabilities distributed among many different companies is enabling complex virtual enterprises to be formed on the fly. A whole new class of software, created by companies like Bowstreet, G5 Technologies, and Hewlett-Packard, is emerging that will form the glue for such plug-and-play organizations. By coding business processes in common protocols, such as XML, this software enables different companies' processes to be easily connected or disconnected to suit their business needs.

Companies that really understand how intelligence migration is reshaping business are often able to better exploit the power of the Internet. Avon is a good case in point. Its first response to the Internet back in 1997 was to launch a site for selling cosmetics directly to customers. The site failed to generate much business—it accounted for only 2% of the company's sales in 1999—and, more important, it felt like a real threat to the company's most valuable asset: its half-million-member independent sales force.

Now, Avon is rethinking its Internet strategy. It is planning to create a site that provides "personal portals" for each of its sales representatives. The reps will use the site to place and track orders, get current information on products, and analyze the buying patterns of their customers—it will, in effect, become the shared "back office" for their individual businesses. Here, again, we see infrastructure intelligence migrating to the core (to Avon) and customer intelligence being pushed to where it can be applied with the highest degree of customization (to the periphery, with the reps). Consolidating the infrastructure provides an important benefit to Avon. One of the company's biggest problems is high turnover among its sales representatives. The reps, who often work part-time, tend to drift in and out of the work force, and when they leave, they take their customer relationships with them. Now, for the first time, Avon will have centralized information about all its end customers. This information will outlive the tenures of the individual representatives and can easily be transferred to new reps.

So what will Avon do with its existing e-commerce site? It will limit its sales to fewer than 500 of the company's 6,000 products. Customers who want any of the other products will be referred to their local Avon rep, who will call on them in person. The site will now support rather than threaten the reps.

## Profiting from Intelligence Migration

In addition to changing the way existing businesses operate, the decoupling and mobilization of network intelligence are opening attractive new business opportunities. Forward-thinking companies are beginning to use four strategies to capitalize on the migration patterns (see "Four Strategies for Profiting from Intelligence Migration" at the end of this article.):

### ARBITRAGE

Because intelligence can be located anywhere on a network, there are often opportunities for moving particular types of intelligence to new regions or countries where the cost of maintaining the intelligence is lower. Such an arbitrage strategy is particularly useful for people-intensive services that can be delivered over a network, because labor costs tend to vary dramatically across geographies. PeopleSupport, for example, operates a large center in Manila that provides live on-line help services to customers of U.S. companies. By transporting the intelligence of a long-distance support staff over the Internet, the company is able to exploit the difference in labor costs between the Philippines and the United States. The arbitrage strategy can also be used for other people-intensive services like medical transcription, market research, transaction processing, and back office support. Countries in the Indian subcontinent, Eastern Europe, and Latin America provide rich pools of low-cost human resources that can be accessed over a network. Additionally, countries like India with a significant English-speaking population and skilled engineering talent can provide specialty engineering services for software development, engineering design, architectural design, and statistical analysis.

## AGGREGATION

As intelligence decouples, companies have the opportunity to combine formerly isolated pools of dedicated infrastructure intelligence into a large pool of shared infrastructure that can be provided over a network. Loudcloud, based in Sunnyvale, California, is an example of an emerging new breed of utility that employs the aggregation strategy. Loudcloud offers "instant" infrastructure to e-businesses by converting the various aspects of intelligence required to operate a Web site into a suite of services called Smart Cloud. Each aspect of intelligence is offered as a distinct service, including a Database Cloud (storage), an Application Server Cloud (processing), a Mail Cloud (dispatch), a Staging Cloud (testing), and an eServices Cloud (applications). The

Smart Cloud services are coordinated by Opsware—an operating environment that automates tasks such as capacity scaling, configuration, service provisioning, and software updating.

Nike used Loudcloud's services to accommodate a dramatic traffic surge on its site during the recent Olympic Games in Australia. Opsware enabled Nike to scale up its computing needs on a temporary, just-in-time basis, allowing it to avoid the complexity and expense of expanding its capacity permanently. As Nike's traffic increased, the site received more server and storage capacity, and when the traffic died down after the Games, Opsware decommissioned the added computers. Loudcloud billed Nike just like a utility does, on the amount of services actually used.

**REWIRING**

The mobilization of intelligence allows organizations to more tightly coordinate processes with many participants. In essence, this strategy involves creating an information network that all participants connect to and establishing an information exchange standard that allows them to communicate. Consider how the start-up e-Trak is rewiring the information chain for the towing of illegally parked vehicles. The towing process involves a complex sequence of interactions among the police officer at the towing site, the dispatcher in the police station, the towing company, and the towing company's drivers. Traditionally, the police officer radios the dispatcher in the police station, who then calls various tow companies. The tow companies in turn radio their drivers to find a suitable truck in the area. Once a truck is located, confirmation is passed from the towing company to the dispatcher and back to the officer. This inefficient process takes a lot of time, during which the officer is forced to remain near the vehicle.

E-Trak sets up an information network that connects law enforcement agencies to towing companies. Police officers initiate a tow request through a radio link or a mobile display terminal connected to a network. The tow information is sent to the e-Trak system, which uses a database to automatically select the best towing company based on availability and proximity. The towing company receives the tow information through an e-Trak terminal in its office, and it communicates with the driver via radio, computer, or pager. The e-Trak system has allowed law enforcement agencies to cut response times from 30 minutes to ten minutes, letting them handle twice as many tows without increasing staff.

## REASSEMBLY

Another new kind of intermediary creates value by aggregating, reorganizing, and configuring disparate pieces of intelligence into coherent, personalized packages for customers. One example of such a reassembler is Yodlee, a start-up that has developed technology to consolidate and summarize information from multiple online sources on one Web site. Users get one-click access to a diverse set of personal information, including bank balances, travel reservations, investments, e-mail, shopping, bills, and calendars, and they can access it from a PC, handheld device, or Web-enabled phone. The Yodlee platform also allows the different pieces of intelligence to communicate with one another by securely and intelligently transmitting personal information across multiple accounts, services, platforms, and devices. For example, severe weather data transmitted to a Web-enabled phone could initiate an automatic call to inquire about potential flight delays for a travel reservation.

## What Managers Need to Do

The migration of intelligence raises different sorts of challenges for different companies. To prepare your company, start by undertaking a straightforward analysis. First, define what intelligence is in your business. List the various types of intelligence that exist in your organization, using the table "Aspects of Intelligence in Networks" as a guide. Think about intelligence that resides in objects, such as software applications, databases, and computer systems, as well as in the skills and knowledge of your people. Next, ask yourself where intelligence lives in your organization. Is it organized by geography, by line of business, or by customer type? Then, ask yourself where intelligence should live—assuming you could connect all your customers, employees, business processes, and trading partners in a seamless network with infinite bandwidth. Is the current location of your company's intelligence the best location?

Think about the decoupling pattern. Are you making compromises by bundling intelligence that is best centralized with intelligence that is best decentralized? Conceptualize your organization as a network with a core (the back end) and a periphery (the front end). At the back end, can you centralize processes that are shared across different business units to create an internal "utility company"? Can you convert dedicated infrastructure into shared infrastructure by pushing some business processes beyond the walls of the organization to external utility companies? At the front end, can you get closer to your customers and partners by pushing intelligence nearer to them? Can you allow your customers, your sales force, and your channel partners to access and process intelligence directly, so that they have the ability to configure and personalize it themselves?

## Aspects of Intelligence in Networks

*The intelligence of a network is its functionality—its ability to distribute, store, assemble, or modify information. Here we break down intelligence into some of its most common forms.*

| Activity | Definition | Physical Analog |
| --- | --- | --- |
| Configuring | arranging information in a way that responds to a need | configurator software |
| Dispatching | moving information from its source to its appropriate destination | router |
| Storing | collecting information so that it can be accessed quickly and easily | database |
| Processing | converting raw information into useful outcomes | microprocessor |
| Interacting | facilitating the exchange of information | keyboard |
| Coordinating | harmonizing activities performed by multiple entities toward a common goal | operating system |
| Learning | using experience to improve the ability to act | expert system |
| Sensing | detecting and interpreting signals in the environment | antenna |

Think about the mobilization pattern. Are there opportunities to connect, combine, and configure isolated pools of intelligence in creative ways? Reconceptualize your business in terms of the sequences of activities that your customers are trying to accomplish. Think about gaps in the information flows needed to support the sequences. Are you currently doing things in time-consuming, manual ways that could easily be automated if the right information were available? Think about opportunities to rewire your information chains by creating a single network for all your partners. And think about how you might aggregate and reassemble pieces of intelligence from different sources in ways that will save your customers time and effort.

By understanding the implications of intelligence migration for your own company, you will be better able to chart a clear-headed strategy in a time of apparent turmoil. Strategy has always been about finding the right position in a chain of value-creating activities—a position that gives you rather than your competitors control over the flow of profits. That hasn't changed. What has changed is the nature of the value chain itself. Increasingly, it takes the form of a network.

---

## Value Trends in the Network Age

IN A NETWORKED WORLD, where everyone and everything is connected, economic value behaves very differently than it does in the traditional, bounded world. Here are four high-level value trends that all companies should be conscious of as they position themselves in the digital economy.

## Value at the Ends

Most economic value will be created at the ends of networks. At the core—the end most distant from users—generic, scale-intensive functions will consolidate. At the periphery—the end closest to users—highly customized connections with customers will be made. This trend pertains not only to technological networks like the Internet but to networks of companies engaged in shared tasks and even to the human networks that exist within companies.

## Value in Common Infrastructure

Elements of infrastructure that were once distributed among different machines, organizational units, and companies will be brought together and operated as utilities. Shared infrastructure will take the form not only of basic computing and data-storage functions but also of common business functions, such as order processing, warehousing and distribution, and even manufacturing and customer service.

## Value in Modularity

Devices, software, organizational capabilities, and business processes will increasingly be restructured as well-defined, self-contained modules that can be quickly and seamlessly connected with other modules. Value will lie in creating modules that can be plugged in to as many different value chains as possible. Companies and individuals will want to distribute their capabilities as broadly as possible rather than protect them as proprietary assets.

## Value in Orchestration

As modularization takes hold, the ability to coordinate among the modules will become the most valuable business skill. Much of the competition in the business world will center on gaining and maintaining the orchestration role for a value chain or an industry.

---

# Network Intelligence in the Public Sector

THE MIGRATION OF NETWORK Intelligence affects more than business. It also affects public sector activities, such as government, national security, and education. Governments, for example, will be challenged to use electronic networks in general and the Internet in particular to deliver information and services to citizens in much more diverse and personalized ways. The monolithic government bureaucracy will shatter, and new forms of distributed government will emerge. Interestingly, some of the most creative governmental applications of the Internet are found in developing nations. One example is the Indian state of Andhra Pradesh, with a population of 70 million. Under the leadership of its cybersavvy chief minister N. Chandrababu Naidu, it is rolling out an "e-government" system that will let citizens pay taxes and fees, apply for licenses and permits, and participate in municipal meetings through their home computers or public Internet kiosks.

The defense establishment will also need to radically reshape itself to adapt to the digital world, where threats to national security tend to be distributed among far-flung terrorist activity "modules" rather than centralized in powerful states. Centralized intelligence will need to be decentralized and dispersed. (Perhaps the CIA will be replaced by the DIA—the Distributed Intelligence

Agency.) And the military will need to be reorganized to emphasize relatively small autonomous units at the edges connected through a network to a central core of coordination and command.

Some of the most radical changes will take place in education. Students will no longer need to come together in centralized institutions to take general courses. Using the intelligence of the Internet, they will able to remotely access modules of education and training content, assembling courses of instruction that respond to their immediate and particular needs. Universities will need to shift from providing generalized just-in-case knowledge to providing customizable just-in-time knowledge.

---

# Four Strategies for Profiting from Intelligence Migration

### Arbitrage
Move intelligence to new regions or countries where the cost of maintaining it is lower.

### Aggregation
Combine formerly isolated pieces of dedicated infrastructure intelligence into a large pool of shared infrastructure that can be provided over a network.

### Rewiring
Connect islands of intelligence by creating a common information backbone.

**Reassembly**

Reorganize pieces of intelligence from diverse sources into coherent, personalized packages for customers.

# Notes

1. See John Hagel and Marc Singer, "Unbundling the Corporation," HBR May–June 1999.

Originally published in January 2001
Reprint R0101E

# The Superefficient Company

MICHAEL HAMMER

## Executive Summary

MOST COMPANIES DO A GREAT JOB promoting efficiency within their own walls, streamlining internal processes wherever possible. But they have less success
coordinating cross-company business interactions.

When data pass between companies, inconsistencies, errors, and misunderstandings routinely arise, leading to wasted work—for instance, the same sales, order
entry, and customer data may be entered repeatedly
into different systems. Typically, scores of employees at
each company manage these cumbersome interactions.
The costs of such inefficiencies are very real and very
large.

In this article, Michael Hammer outlines the activities
and goals used in streamlining cross-company processes. He breaks down the approach into four stages:
*scoping*—identifying the business process for redesign

199

and selecting a partner; *organizing*—establishing a joint committee to oversee the redesign and convening a design team to implement it; *redesigning*—taking apart and reassembling the process, with performance goals in mind; and *implementing*—rolling out the new process and communicating it across the collaborating companies.

The author describes how several companies have streamlined their supply-chain and product development processes. Plastics compounder Geon integrated its forecasting and fulfillment processes with those of its main supplier after watching inventories, working capital, and shipping times creep up. General Mills coordinated the delivery of its yogurt with Land O'Lakes; butter and yogurt travel cost effectively in the same trucks to the same stores.

Hammer says this new kind of collaboration promises to change the traditional vocabulary of corporate relationships. What if you and I sell different products to the same customer? We're not competitors, but what are we? In the past, we didn't care. Now, we should, the author says.

---

Having fought your way through the productivity wars of the past ten years, you're probably proud of the leanness of your operations. And rightly so. You've revamped your processes, reducing overhead and cutting out redundant activities. You've enhanced the quality of your products and services, ridding your organization of mistakes and miscommunication. And you've broken down the walls between your units, getting people to work together and share information. In short, you've created a truly efficient company.

Guess what? You've only just begun.

While it's true that companies have done a great job streamlining their internal processes, it's equally true that their shared processes—those that involve interactions with other companies—are largely a mess. Think about your procurement process. It's the mirror image of your supplier's order-fulfillment process, with many of the same tasks and information requirements. When your purchasing agent fills out a requisition form, for instance, she is performing essentially the same work that the supplier's order-entry clerk performs when he takes the order. Yet there's probably little or no coordination between the two processes. Even if you and your supplier exchange transaction data electronically, the actual work is still performed in isolation, separated by a very deep intercompany divide.

Because cross-company processes are not coordinated, a vast number of activities end up being duplicated. The same information is entered repeatedly into different systems, the same forms are filled out and passed around multiple times, the same checks and certifications are done over and over. When activities and data make the jump between companies, inconsistencies, errors, and misunderstandings routinely arise, leading to even more wasted work. And scores of employees typically have to be assigned to manage the cumbersome interactions between companies. Though all these inefficiencies may be hidden from your accounting systems, which track only what happens within your own walls, the costs are real, and they are large. Today, efficiency ends at the edges of a company.

Streamlining cross-company processes is the next great frontier for reducing costs, enhancing quality, and speeding operations. It's where this decade's productivity

wars will be fought. The victors will be those companies
that are able to take a new approach to business, working closely with partners to design and manage processes
that extend across traditional corporate boundaries.
They will be the ones that make the leap from efficiency
to superefficiency.

## Tearing Down Walls

To get a clearer view of the prodigious costs of uncoordi-
nated intercompany processes—and the great rewards of
integrating them—look at the recent experiences of
Geon, a chemical company based in Ohio. Geon spun off
from BFGoodrich in 1993. Through organic growth and a
series of acquisitions and joint ventures, it established
itself as the world's largest producer of polyvinyl compound (PVC), garnering revenues of $1.3 billion in 1999.
(Last year, Geon merged with another chemical company, M.A. Hanna, to form PolyOne.)

Through most of the 1990s, Geon was a vertically integrated business. It bought chlorine and ethylene and
combined them to create the basic raw material for PVC,
vinyl chloride monomer (VCM). It then transformed
VCM into resins and, through a series of additional
steps, into various compounds used in products ranging
from computer housings to home appliances. Like many
industrial companies, Geon focused its energies in the
mid-1990s on breaking down the walls between its units
in order to reduce costs and create greater value for customers. The company followed a program that is by now
familiar: integrating and simplifying core business processes and installing an ERP system to support them. By
allowing information and transactions to flow more easily among different parts of the company, Geon profited

handsomely. The percentage of orders shipped on time soared, customer complaints almost vanished, the need to pay premium freight rates to make up for scheduling foul-ups evaporated, inventory levels fell sharply, and overall productivity got a strong boost. Geon's costs dropped by tens of millions of dollars, and its working capital fell from more than 16% of sales to less than 14%.

Then, in 1999, the company initiated a major strategic shift: Recognizing that it did not have the sales volumes necessary to produce VCM and resins at a competitive cost, the company decided to focus entirely on the compounding side of the business. Producing compounds was a higher-value-adding activity, and it was less dependent on scale and more reliant on clever engineering to meet specific customer needs. This new focus would give Geon the opportunity to gain a true competitive advantage and to widen its margins. In support of the new strategy, Geon divested its VCM and resins operations to a joint venture with Occidental Chemical called OxyVinyls, which became its primary supplier of materials.

While Geon's actions were strategically sound, they were operationally disastrous. In effect, Geon erected a high (intercompany) wall where it had just demolished a low (intracompany) one. VCM and resin production had only recently been integrated with compounding, and now they were again torn asunder, this time becoming parts of separate companies. The results were all too predictable: Work was no longer coordinated, information was no longer shared, and overhead and duplication were reintroduced. Expediters, schedulers, and a host of clerical personnel had to be hired to manage the interface between Geon and OxyVinyls. Data had to be entered twice, resulting in an 8% error rate on orders that Geon placed with OxyVinyls—wrong purchase-order numbers, product numbers, prices, and so on. The time needed to process orders also jumped as communications became more formal and interfaces more complex.

On the production side, as Geon and OxyVinyls became less aware of each other's inventories, shipments, and levels of demand, their manufacturing processes became more irregular, requiring many stops and starts, delays, and unexpected changeovers. Geon's horizon for production planning was dramatically foreshortened, from about seven weeks to about three. Its inventories increased 15%, its working capital went up 12%, and its order-fulfillment cycle time tripled. Not only had Geon lost the earlier benefits it had gained by painstakingly integrating its business processes, but in many ways the situation became even worse than it had been before Geon's internal wall-bashing.

Geon's problems may appear particularly dire, but they were actually no worse than those faced by most companies. There was, however, one crucial difference: Geon saw them. Its rapidly decaying performance underscored to management the huge penalties of disjointed intercompany processes. Rather than ignoring the inefficiency or dismissing it as the inevitable consequence of working with other companies, Geon took action. It worked closely with OxyVinyls to connect both companies' processes and the computer systems that supported them.

The two companies tightly integrated their forecasting process; now, as soon as Geon uses information from its customers to predict demand for compounds, that forecast is transmitted, over the Internet, to OxyVinyls, which incorporates it into its own forecast for resins and monomers. Ordering and fulfillment processes are also tightly knit. Within 24 hours of receiving an order from one of its customers, Geon translates the order into the materials it will need from OxyVinyls and automatically dispatches an order directly into OxyVinyls' fulfillment process and system. In turn, order acknowledgments and confirmations, advance shipment notifications, and invoices automatically go from OxyVinyls back to Geon.

The jobs and behavior of employees involved in the processes have changed significantly as a result. Production planners in one company, for example, no longer have to waste time trying to find out what's going on in another company. Instead, they can concentrate on solving problems in ways that benefit both companies. When there are tight markets for raw materials, for instance, planners from Geon and OxyVinyls work hand-in-hand to reschedule production runs and shipments to ensure that plant capacity is used as efficiently as possible. Geon's people also better appreciate that small orders increase OxyVinyls' shipping costs, and they now look for opportunities to consolidate purchases. They know that when OxyVinyls' costs go down, so do the prices of the products it sells to Geon.

Performance measures have also changed. Geon's purchasing agents used to be evaluated primarily on the prices they negotiated for materials. Even though the availability of materials is critical to manufacturing productivity, that factor was not taken into account in assessing the agents because it was assumed they had little knowledge of or control over the supplier's shipments. Now that the agents have accurate information about OxyVinyls' production and shipping schedules, they are held accountable for the availability as well as the price of the materials they buy.

Geon has recently gone a step further, integrating its processes with those of its customers. It has put sensors into some of its major buyers' warehouses so that it always knows how much of its compounds a customer has in stock. When inventories decline to an agreed-upon level, Geon automatically sends replenishments, cutting out many traditional stock-checking and ordering activities.

Through Geon's efforts, the processes of three different companies—the customer's procurement processes, Geon's order-fulfillment and procurement processes, and OxyVinyls' order-fulfillment process—have been integrated. They are now all managed as a single process, without regard to corporate boundaries and with much less friction, over-

*Companies are starting to see business processes—and manage them—as they truly are: chains of activities that are performed by different organizations.*

head, and error. The payoffs have been dramatic. Geon's 8% error rate in placing orders has gone to 0%, its order-fulfillment cycle time has fallen back to its earlier level, and its inventories have declined 15%. Its labor costs have also fallen, because non-value-adding work has been eliminated. More important, the company has been able to reassign many of its people to jobs in which they serve customers rather than just fix mistakes. That's enabled Geon to better fulfill its new strategy of focusing on high-value-added activities.

## Relocating Work

It may be tempting to look at Geon's story simply as an illustration of the power of using the Internet to connect disparate information systems. But while that's an accurate technological description, it misses the bigger point: Separate processes in separate companies have been connected and combined and now work as one. New technologies may be the glue, but the more important innovation is the change in the way people think and work. Rather than seeing business processes as ending at the edges of their companies, Geon and its partners now see them—and manage them—as they truly are: chains of activities that are performed by different organizations.

Although the concept of supply chain integration has been around for some time now, companies have had trouble making it a reality. In most cases, that's because they've viewed it as merely a technological challenge rather than as what it really is: a process and management challenge. Once you adopt this broader view, you can quickly cut a lot of costs and waste from your existing operations. But you can do much more as well—you can discover new and better ways to work. You can begin to shift activities across corporate boundaries. If your company, for instance, happens to be in a better position today to do some work that my company has traditionally done, then you should do it—even if that work is "officially" my responsibility. The increased costs you incur doing the work will be more than offset by the benefits of improving the process as a whole, benefits that will accrue to both of us.

IBM is now using this approach to manage customers' orders. In 1998, IBM estimated that it spent $233 to handle each order it received, much of which went to "order management"—getting the order in, making sure that it was at the appropriate price, answering customers' questions about payment status, and so on. The overhead could be traced in large part to the wall that separated IBM from its customers. The company had long required that all customer interactions be mediated by an IBM

employee—usually, a sales rep. By removing this requirement, IBM has been able to integrate its fulfillment process with its customers' procurement processes and
redesign the unified process to work much more efficiently and flexibly. Now customers can do for themselves much of the work that IBM had previously done
for them, with greater convenience and lower costs. With
the new process and systems, customers can enter their
own orders into IBM's computer system and can check
the status of their orders. IBM wins because its costs are
lower; the customers win because they get the work done
correctly at a time of their choosing, and they are spared
the bureaucratic burden of interacting with IBM's gate-
keepers. There are other benefits as well. One important
set of customers—value-adding resellers—has been able
to reduce its inventories of IBM equipment by more than
30%. Since the resellers can get orders into IBM's process
more quickly and can find out when the orders will actually be filled, they get by with less stock on hand. That
makes them happier customers, which IBM knows
makes them more loyal customers. It also reduces channel inventory, tempering the risk that IBM will be
harmed by sudden shifts in demand.

At the same time, IBM is now doing some work that
customers used to have to do for themselves. The large
corporations that buy from IBM typically standardize
the computers they use, requiring all employees to order
the same configuration. But in practice, many people
get the specifications wrong or make other mistakes in
ordering; it was not uncommon for IBM to see an error
rate of more than 50% in orders from corporate customers. In effect, the customer's ordering process was
defective (in not screening out inappropriate orders),
and IBM had to compensate for the failure. Now, IBM

has taken over the work of vetting customer orders. The customer provides IBM with a complete description of the approved configuration. IBM then limits the customer's employees to ordering only that configuration. Both IBM and the customer benefit because they have to spend less time cleaning up the mess that results from inaccurate orders.

## Simplifying Supply Chains

Another high-tech company, Hewlett-Packard, has taken an even more aggressive approach to restructuring work in cross-company processes—in a way that is reshaping the economics of its supply chain for computer monitors. A typical purchaser of an HP monitor probably has no idea how many companies are involved in producing it. Like most computer makers, HP has outsourced much of its manufacturing to contract producers, such as Solectron and Celestica. The contract manufacturer buys the case for the monitor from an injection molder, which acquires the material used to make the case from a plastics compounder (Geon is an example), which in turn buys the material for the compound from a resin maker. This supply chain is fairly easy to describe, but, until recently, it was almost impossible to manage.

For one thing, the suppliers at the opposite end of the chain from HP had no idea how many monitors HP would actually need; they often didn't even know that HP was the ultimate destination for their resin or compound. Consequently, each had to carry a lot of inventory in case an HP order came barreling down the chain. In many cases, the inventory that they did carry ended up not being what HP needed at the moment. When that happened, HP was sometimes unable to deliver an order when the customer needed it, forcing the customer to go elsewhere. Disputes between upstream suppliers could also lead to unexpected delivery delays that might disrupt HP's ability to fulfill orders. Such situations meant lost revenue for everyone in the supply chain.

Another complexity was the volatility in order specifications. In theory, once HP placed an order, its suppliers should have been ready to roll. But the reality of the computer business is that nothing stays fixed for long. On average, an order for a batch of computer monitors changes four times before it is completely filled, usually in response to shifts in marketplace demand. Quantity, delivery date, and color are just a few of the variables that are routinely altered.

The disparity in scale between the participants in this supply chain complicated matters further. HP and its resin supplier are giant companies, and the contract manufacturers are fairly substantial as well. But most injection molders are relatively small outfits, as are most compounders. So every HP order for monitor cases was usually split among many compounders, each of which bought resin in relatively small volumes—and, consequently, at relatively high prices—from the resin maker. HP's potential purchasing clout, in other words, dissipated at each step in the chain that separated it from its ultimate supplier. Because it was shielded from the suppliers of compounds and resins, HP also lacked the ability to track their quality and delivery performance and their prices and terms, and it rarely heard their ideas for enhancing products and processes.

*When processes are linked, any change to an order ripples through the entire supply chain.*

An army of people, dispersed among the different companies and using a host of unrelated information systems, was required to hold this cumbersome set of processes together—at great cost. Recognizing the problem, HP in 1999 resolved to integrate the entire supply chain and coordinate the unified process. The company assumed responsibility for ensuring that all parties work together, share information, and operate in a way that guarantees the lowest costs and the highest levels of availability throughout the chain.

The hub of the newly integrated process is a computer system that HP set up to share information among all the participants. HP posts its demand forecasts and revisions for its partners to use in their own forecasting. The partners post their plans and schedules and use the system to communicate with their own suppliers and customers, exchanging electronic orders, acknowledgments, and invoices. HP's procurement staff manages the entire process, monitoring the performance of the upstream suppliers, helping to resolve disputes relating to payments, and keeping supply and demand in balance. The company's purchasing agents, once narrowly focused on terms and conditions, have seen their jobs broaden considerably.

The integrated process has dramatically enhanced the performance of the supply chain. Today, any kind of change to an HP order ripples through the chain instantaneously, allowing everyone to react quickly. And if any problem crops up that threatens HP's ability to meet its forecasts, HP learns of it early enough to make other plans. Because it coordinates the entire process, HP can also order all its required resin directly from the resin supplier. It provides the resin maker with an aggregate order, and it receives a single bill at a uniform, considerably lower contract price. The resin maker benefits from this new relationship as well; it gets the simplicity and security of dealing with one large customer rather than a host of small ones.

Streamlining the supply process has helped every participant, but HP has perhaps profited most. In the first implementation of this process, the price HP pays for its resins has gone down as much as 5%, the number of people it requires to manage the supply chain has been cut in half, and the time it takes to fill an order for a computer monitor has dropped 25%. Best of all, HP estimates that it is increasing sales in the areas in which it has implemented this newly integrated process by 2%. These are sales that the company had previously lost because it could not deliver the right product at the right time. HP no longer has to commit the mortal sin of turning customers away.

## From Coordination to Collaboration

The examples I've described so far center on the management of supply chains. That shouldn't be a surprise. Supply chain problems are highly disruptive—and costly—to companies, and fixing them delivers a big, immediate payoff. So companies have tended to focus their initial efforts in streamlining cross-company processes on the supply chain. But tantalizing opportunities in other areas are now starting to appear. The next major wave is likely to be the integration of product-development processes. A company, its suppliers, and even its customers will begin to share information and activities to speed the design of a product and raise the odds of its success in the market. Suppliers, for example, will be able to begin developing components before an overall product design is complete, and they will also be able to provide early feedback as to whether components can be produced within specified cost and time constraints. Customers, for their part, will be able to review the product as it evolves and provide input on how it meets their needs. In a very real sense, this kind of collaborative product development will be the multicompany analogue of concurrent engineering, which has transformed internal product development over the past 15 years.

On a more profound level, we're beginning to see examples of an entirely new kind of process collaboration, which promises to change the way we think and even talk about business. The traditional vocabulary of corporate relationships is meager: If you sell me something, I am your customer, and you are my supplier; if another company tries to sell me the same thing, it is your competitor. And that's about it, because those were the only relationships that made any difference to us. But what if you and I are both buying the same product or service from the same supplier? In the past, it was unlikely that either of us would discover that we had such a relationship, and, even if we did, the information would have been of little, if any, value. Consequently, we had no term to describe it. Similarly, what if you and I sell different products, but to the same customer? We are not competitors, but what are we? In the past, we didn't care. Now, we should.

Consider the recent experience of General Mills, a giant in the business of consumer packaged goods, with brands ranging from Cheerios to Yoplait. For years, margins have been falling for consumer packaged goods as distribution channels have consolidated and consumers have become more selective. Through the 1990s, General

Mills led the industry in squeezing costs out of its supply chain. Through increased purchasing effectiveness, manufacturing productivity, and distribution efficiencies, General Mills' cost per case of product declined by a remarkable 10% during the decade. But as a new decade dawned, the company's leaders realized they would have to move beyond the confines of their linear supply chain in order to find new cost-savings opportunities. Among their first ideas was a radical new approach to the distribution of their refrigerated products, like yogurt.

As businesses, refrigerated goods and dry goods have very different characteristics. The top seven dry-goods manufacturers together account for nearly 40% of total supermarket sales in that category. Each of the manufacturers has enough sales to efficiently operate its own distribution network, including warehouses and trucks. In the refrigerated category, however, the top seven players represent less than 15% of total supermarket sales, and nearly all lack the scale needed for a highly efficient, dedicated distribution network. Nonetheless, each company maintains one, and, unsurprisingly, each suffers from suboptimal productivity as a result.

When a refrigerated truck laden with Yoplait, for example, leaves a General Mills warehouse headed for local supermarkets, it is often carrying less than a full load. Even more often, it is carrying orders for several supermarkets, requiring it to make many stops. If the truck is delayed in traffic or encounters a snafu at one of its early stops, it may not make it to the final supermarket on its route that day. If that supermarket has just run an ad promoting a special on Yoplait, it will have to deal with angry consumers, and General Mills will face a frustrated supermarket in addition to lost sales.

General Mills realized that it could address the problem by integrating its distribution process with another company's. It found the perfect partner in Land O'Lakes, a large producer of butter and margarine. Land O'Lakes products do not compete with those of General Mills, but they have the same warehousing and transport requirements and the same customers. The two companies agreed to combine their distribution networks, giving them the scale necessary for high efficiency. Today, General Mills yogurt and Land O'Lakes butter ride in the same trucks on their way to the same supermarkets. When Land O'Lakes receives an order, it ships the goods to a General Mills facility, where they are immediately loaded onto a truck containing General Mills yogurt headed for the same customer. Or, if the customer chooses to pick up the goods itself, the orders are stored together in a special section of a General Mills warehouse.

With the combined process, General Mills' trucks go out much fuller than before, and since they're delivering more products to each supermarket, they make fewer stops and suffer fewer delays. The arrangement has been so successful, in terms of both lower costs and higher customer satisfaction, that the two manufacturers are now planning to integrate their order-taking and billing processes as well. They are also working together to create incentives for customers to order larger combined amounts from the two companies, which will result in even greater transport savings.

General Mills and Land O'Lakes are noncompetitive suppliers—what I've come to call *cosuppliers*—to the same customers, and it is to their mutual advantage to find ways to work together. The potential for such relationships has always existed, but in the past it was difficult, if not impossible, to make them work. There was simply no efficient means of sharing information quickly and accurately enough. Manually coordinating two companies' deliveries through a shared distribution network would quickly have turned into a logistical nightmare. But with the Internet and associated communications technologies, these kinds of business relationships suddenly become feasible, opening up new opportunities for creative companies.

Indeed, anywhere that different companies use similar resources, there are opportunities for reducing costs through sharing. For instance, a recent study by a group of manufacturers showed that they collectively owned about 30 million square feet of warehouse facilities in the greater Chicago area, but only 82% of the space was being used. By sharing warehouse space with one another, these companies envision eliminating the waste

*No matter how tough it is to get different departments to work together, getting different companies to collaborate is even harder.*

and sharing the benefits. The U.S. trucking fleet is plagued by similar inefficiencies. Because shippers plan their deliveries independently, they often have to pay for drivers to move empty trucks from the end point of one trip to the start of the next one. At any given time, 20% of the nation's trucks are traveling empty, raising costs for both shippers and truckers. Some companies, however, are now starting to merge their logistics processes. By planning shipments and contracting for trucks together, they're saving money for themselves and their carriers.

## Making It Happen

Companies that have redesigned their internal processes know that success requires a rigorous, structured approach. The same is true for streamlining cross-company processes, but here the challenges are even greater. No matter how tough it is to get different departments to work together, getting different companies to collaborate is even harder. I have found that it's best to structure the project into four major stages: scoping, organizing, redesigning, and implementing. (See "Four Steps to Superefficiency.")

### SCOPING

First, you have to set your sights on the right targets. Start by identifying the intercompany process that offers the greatest opportunity for improving your overall business performance, whether it's a supply chain, product development, distribution, or other process. Typically, you'll want to select a process that you've already brought to peak internal efficiency; it makes little sense to merge processes that still harbor inefficiencies.

The choice of the partner you'll work with may be the most important decision you'll make. Obviously, the partner needs to be a company that is likely to have an interest in working with you to streamline the process, but that is not nearly enough. You need to evaluate the other company's technical competence and cultural fit for doing intercompany process redesign. Does it have significant experience with transforming its internal processes? It should, since a cross-company process is a risky place to learn the basics. Can the company make decisions quickly? If not, the effort will never yield fruit. Does it have a collaborative style? A focus on the short term rather than the long term, a predilection for contracts rather than trust, a search for one-sided advantage rather than mutual benefit—any of these will doom the initiative.

# Four Steps to Superefficiency

Streamlining cross-company business processes is the next great frontier for reducing costs, enhancing quality, and speeding operations. But the leap to superefficiency requires a rigorous, structured approach such as the one described here.

| Stage | 1. Scoping | | 2. Organizing | |
|---|---|---|---|---|
| **Activities** | Identify the appropriate business process to redesign | Select a partner | Establish an executive steering committee | Convene a design team |
| **Keys to Success** | The process should offer substantial opportunities to enhance overall business performance, and it should already be operating at peak internal efficiency. | The partner should have a strong interest in the initiative; be experienced with internal process redesign; make decisions quickly; and have a collaborative culture. | The steering committee should convene early and should include leaders from both companies. The committee should define each company's investments, roles, and share of benefits; establish procedures for resolving disputes; and establish performance measures and goals. | The design team should have between six and 12 members committed full-time to the project. The team should include members from both companies and should include experts in existing processes, in process redesign, and in change management. |

| Stage | 3. Redesigning | 4. Implementing | |
|---|---|---|---|
| **Activities** | Design the new, integrated process in a way that fulfills performance goals | Roll out the new process | Communicate |
| **Keys to Success** | The redesign effort should follow these principles:<br>• The final customer comes first.<br>• The entire process should be designed as a unit.<br>• No activity should be performed more than once.<br>• Work should be done by whoever is in the best position to do it.<br>• The entire process should operate with one database. | The process rollout should occur in clearly defined stages, it should focus on achieving benefits early, and it should move quickly to maintain momentum. | Communications should occur regularly, reach everyone in both companies, emphasize the rationale and expected benefits of the project, and define expectations for every employee. |

## ORGANIZING

The operating and cultural consequences of intercompany process redesign are so far-reaching that strong
executive leadership is needed from the outset. An executive steering committee, comprising leaders from both
companies, should be convened very early. One of its first
responsibilities should be to define the rules of engagement. What will each party invest in this effort? How will
benefits be shared? How will conflicts and disputes be
resolved? Collaboration on processes is fairly unfamiliar
territory for most organizations, and setting ground
rules at the start will avoid a lot of misunderstanding
later. The steering committee also needs to decide which
performance measures (such as cycle times, transaction
costs, or inventory levels) will be targeted for improvement and to establish specific, quantified goals.

While the steering committee sponsors the process
redesign, it does not actually do it. That is the role of the
design team. The design team should include people from
both companies, and its core members should be experts
in the existing process, people skilled in process redesign,
and specialists in technology and change management.
Too large a team is unwieldy, and too small a group lacks
the critical mass to get anything done; typically, six to 12
people is the right size. As a rule, all members should be
assigned full time to the project. Speed is of the essence
here, and part-timers tend to be so distracted by other
responsibilities that they move glacially, if at all.

## REDESIGNING

During the redesign stage, the team members roll up
their sleeves, take the existing process apart, and
reassemble it to achieve the performance goals. Here are

some principles that the team should follow in coming up with the new design:

- **The final customer comes first.** Both companies need to submerge their narrower goals in service to a higher one: meeting the needs of the customer whom they work together to serve. Participants must remember that a company they have always considered a customer may, in fact, be merely a collaborator in serving the ultimate customer.

- **The entire process should be designed as a unit.** That may sound obvious, but it's an easy point to lose sight of. Make sure all members stay focused on the big picture; otherwise, they may begin to address the process in pieces rather than as a whole.

- **No activity should be performed more than once.** Eliminating duplicated activities is one of the best ways to make intercompany process redesign pay off quickly—and that's crucial to building and maintaining momentum.

- **Work should be done by whoever is in the best position to do it.** IBM enforces its customers' computer standards; HP buys resin for its suppliers' suppliers' suppliers. It defeats the purpose of a collaborative to attempt to be self-sufficient. Do what you do best, and let others do the same.

- **The entire process should operate with one database.** When everyone shares the same version of all the information, reconciliation tasks can be eliminated and assets can be deployed precisely and efficiently.

Working on an interdisciplinary process design team is an unfamiliar experience for almost everyone; when

one's teammates come from another company and not
just another department, the unfamiliarity increases dramatically. Frequently, people from one company will lack
even the most basic understanding of the operations and
concerns of the other. Team members therefore need to
develop an appreciation for the challenges facing the
other company. They must also learn that they are not
representing their company's interests but those of the
process as a whole.

## IMPLEMENTING

Once the process has been redesigned, it must be rolled
out. Two principles are critical to success in this stage.
The first is "think big, start small, move fast." Trying to
implement a radically new process in one step is almost
always a recipe for disaster. Any intercompany working
relationship will be tenuous until real results are
achieved, and the longer it takes to reach that milestone,
the greater the risk that the whole thing will unravel.
Consequently, the entire effort must be conducted with
an eye on the clock. The redesign team should develop
its vision for the process being revamped in weeks, not
months, and it should organize the implementation so as
to deliver tangible results quickly.

The second principle is "communicate relentlessly."
Redesigning an intercompany process not only changes
people's jobs, it also changes how they think about and
relate to other companies. Information sharing, openness, and trust need to replace information hoarding,
suspicion, and downright hostility. Without constant
reminders of the rationale for the redesign, the benefits
that will accrue to each company, and the expectations
for every employee, the needed cultural change simply
will not occur.

It's natural for a company to get nervous about tearing down the walls that enclose its organization. The act goes against many long-held notions of corporate identity and strategy. But most companies were nervous about breaking down the walls between their internal departments and business units, too. Some even delayed the effort—and they have spent the last decade playing catch-up with their competitors. Streamlining intercompany processes isn't just an interesting idea; it's the next frontier of efficiency. Right now, it's the best way to develop a performance advantage over your competitors—or to prevent them from developing one over you.

Originally published in September 2001
Reprint R0108E

# About the Contributors

**PHILIP BROMILEY** holds the Curtis L. Carlson Chair in Strategic Management at the University of Minnesota. He has served on the editorial boards of *Academy of Management Journal* and *Organization Science* and currently serves on the boards of *Strategic Management Journal* and *Strategy and Organization*. He is an associate editor for *Management Science*. His current research examines the microstructure of competition, the behavioral foundations of strategic management research, and corporate risk-taking in R&D.

**ROBERT BROWN** is the Morse-Alumni Distinguished Teaching Professor in the University of Minnesota's Department of Cultural Studies and Comparative Literature, where he directs their graduate programs. Trained as an anthropological linguist and rhetorician, he now works on the relationships among language, culture, power, and consciousness in everyday life—how we talk, write, and think, and why it matters so much.

**KATHLEEN M. EISENHARDT** is a professor of strategy and organization at the School of Engineering, Stanford University, and research director of the Stanford Technology Ventures Program. Her research and teaching focus on managing in high-velocity, intensely competitive markets. Her awards include the Pacific Telesis Foundation award for her ideas on fast strategic decision making, the Whittemore Prize for her writing on organizing global firms in rapidly changing markets, the *Administrative Science Quarterly* Scholarly Contribution Award for her work on product innovation, and the George R. Terry Book Award for her book, *Competing on the Edge: Strategy as Structured Chaos*, coauthored with Shona L. Brown. She is a fellow of the academy of management and the world economic forum.

ORIT GADIESH is widely acknowledged as an expert on management and corporate strategy. As Chairman of the Board of Bain & Company, Ms. Gadiesh has worked with hundreds of CEOs and senior executives of major international companies on implementing change within the corporation, structuring and managing portfolios, developing and implementing global strategy, executing turnarounds, improving organizational effectiveness, determining channel strategy, and designing cost reduction programs. Ms. Gadiesh has published several articles in the *Harvard Business Review* and is a contributor to The Drucker Foundation's collection *The Organization of the Future*. She is a regular speaker at high-level executive conferences such as the World Economic Forum in Davos, Switzerland and Asia, the Executive Leadership Forum, and the Strategic Leadership Forum. She is also a regular participant of the Bilderberg Meetings. Prior to joining Bain & Company, Ms. Gadiesh served in the office of the Deputy Chief of Staff of the Israeli Army, and has held faculty positions with Hebrew University and the Jerusalem Institute of Management.

JAMES L. GILBERT is a director and vice president of Bain & Company and is currently based in their Munich office. A leader in developing strategy for health care, financial services, media, automotive, telecommunications, and food/consumer products industries, Mr. Gilbert has assisted clients in portfolio and business unit strategy, global strategy and international penetration, new business development and technology management, and cost reduction and re-engineering. A frequent speaker to senior management groups, he is the author of a number of articles on strategy. Mr. Gilbert currently serves on Bain & Company's global nominating committee and in the past he has served on both Bain's global policy committee and compensation and promotion committee. He is also a co-leader of Bain & Company's global health care and global media practice groups.

MICHAEL HAMMER is the founder of Hammer and Company, a management education firm based in Cambridge, Massachusetts.

ROBERT S. KAPLAN is the Marvin Bower Professor of Leadership Development at Harvard Business School. Formerly he was on the faculty of the Graduate School of Industrial Administration, Carnegie Mellon University, where he also served as Dean from 1977 to 1983. He is the creator of the Harvard Business School video series *Measuring Corporate Performance* and the author or coauthor of more than 120 papers and ten books, including, with David Norton, *The Strategy-Focused Organization* and *The Balanced Scorecard*. Dr. Kaplan consults on the design of performance and cost management systems with leading companies worldwide. His research, teaching, consulting, and speaking focus on linking strategy to cost and performance management systems, primarily the Balanced Scorecard and Activity-Based Costing. He is the recipient of numerous honors, including the Outstanding Educator Award from the American Accounting Association and the Chartered Institute of Management Accountants (UK) Award for "Outstanding Contributions to the Accountancy Profession." Dr. Kaplan serves as Chairman of the Balanced Scorecard Collaborative. He can be reached at rkaplan@hbs.edu.

**DAVID P. NORTON** is president of Balanced Scorecard
Collaborative, Inc., a professional services firm that facili-
tates the worldwide awareness, use, enhancement, and
integrity of the Balanced Scorecard. Previously he was the
president of Renaissance Solutions, Inc., a consulting firm he
cofounded in 1992, and of Nolan, Norton & Company, where
he spent seventeen years as president. Dr. Norton is a management consultant, researcher, and speaker in the field of
strategic performance management. With Robert Kaplan, he
is the cocreator of the Balanced Scorecard concept, coauthor
of four *Harvard Business Review* articles, and coauthor of *The
Balanced Scorecard*. He is a trustee of Worcester Polytechnic
Institute and a former director of ACME (the Association of
Consulting Management Engineers). He can be reached at
dnorton@bscol.com.

**DEVAL (DAVE) PARIKH** is an independent consultant to
the high-tech industry. Most recently, Mr. Parikh was a management consultant with Pittigglio Rabin Todd & McGrath
(PRTM), a leading consulting firm to technology-based businesses. At PRTM, he advised clients ranging from *Fortune* 500
to emerging technology companies in the semiconductor,
telecom, and wireless space on supply chain and product
development issues. Prior to joining PRTM, Dave cofounded a
satellite-based, data networking solutions firm in India. Dave
also worked as a process engineer at VLSI Technology (Philips
Semiconductor), where he was responsible for developing
leading edge process technologies for manufacturing ASICs.

**MICHAEL E. PORTER** is the Bishop William Lawrence University Professor at the Institute for Strategy and Competitiveness, based at the Harvard Business School. He is a leading
authority on competitive strategy and international competitiveness. The author of sixteen books and over seventy-five
articles, Professor Porter's ideas have guided economic policy

throughout the world. Professor Porter has led competitiveness initiatives in nations and states such as Canada, India, New Zealand, and Connecticut; guides regional projects in Central America and the Middle East; and is cochairman of the Global Competitiveness Report. In 1994, Professor Porter founded the Initiative for a Competitive Inner City, a nonprofit private sector initiative formed to catalyze business development in distressed inner cities across the United States. The holder of eight honorary doctorates, Professor Porter has won numerous awards for his books, articles, public service, and influence on several fields.

MOHANBIR SAWHNEY is the McCormick Tribune Professor of Electronic Commerce & Technology at the Kellogg School of Management. Professor Sawhney is a globally recognized expert in e-business strategy and technology marketing. *Business Week* named him one of the twenty-five most influential people in e-business. His research on technology, e-business, and marketing has appeared in *California Management Review, Harvard Business Review, Management Science, Marketing Science*, and *Journal of the Academy of Marketing Science*. He also writes extensively for the trade press in publications such as *CIO Magazine, Financial Times, Business 2.0*, and *Context Magazine*. He is the coauthor of *The Seven Steps to Nirvana* and *Techventure: New Rules on Value and Profit from Silicon Valley*. Professor Sawhney has received several awards for teaching excellence, including the Outstanding Professor of the Year at Kellogg in 1998, and the Sidney Levy Award for Excellence in Teaching in 1999 and 1995. He is a fellow of the World Economic Forum, a fellow at Diamond-Cluster International, and a member of Merrill Lynch's Tech-Brains Advisory Board.

At the time this article was originally published, GORDON SHAW was executive director of planning and international at 3M in St. Paul, Minnesota, and past president of the Conference Board's Council of Strategic Planning Executives.

DONALD N. SULL is an assistant professor of business administration in the entrepreneurial management area of the Harvard Business School. Professor Sull's research explores how strong commitments lock firms into the status quo and also provide a tool for managers to successfully overcome corporate inertia. His book on overcoming inertia is scheduled for publication in January 2003. Prior to joining the Harvard faculty, Sull served as an assistant professor at the London Business School where he won the school's Best Teacher Award.

PETER TUFANO is the Sylvan C. Coleman Professor of Financial Management at Harvard Business School. He studies how corporations can use the techniques of corporate engineering to create value in a wide range of business situations, including risk management, security design, and new methods of valuing businesses. He has created and taught a successful MBA and Executive Education course on corporate financial engineering, some of which appears in his text, *Cases in Financial Engineering*, which he coauthored with other HBS faculty. Professor Tufano has also published his work in a wide range of academic and managerial journals and consults to firms on risk management and financial engineering. His work on risk management practices in the gold mining industry was awarded the Smith Breeden prize for the best paper published in the *Journal of Finance*.

# Index